KEEPING UP WITH THE WAR GOD

Taiwan, As It Seemed To Me

by Steven Crook

Yushan Publications
2001

KEEPING UP WITH THE WAR GOD
- TAIWAN, AS IT SEEMED TO ME
by Steven Crook

For my parents

YUSHAN PUBLICATIONS
135 Crescent Drive North
Woodingdean
Brighton BN2 6SG
UK

E-mail: yushan@gmx.net

ISBN 0-9540873-0-5

Printed in Taiwan

Contents

Foreword   5
KEEPING UP WITH THE WAR GOD   7
TAIPEI   11
SEX, MONEY AND POLITICS   23
TREATY PORTS   38
DEAD PRESIDENTS   44
JADE MOUNTAIN   49
DEER HARBOR   62
PEIKANG'S CHAOTIENGONG   67
TAINAN   70
HUNGRY GHOSTS AND HELL MARRIAGES   86
CINEMA FOR THE GODS   95
BLOOD AND RITUAL   108
THE UNITY WAY   114
HEAD-HUNTERS AND CANNIBALS   118
THE EAST   126

Foreword

No thesis drives this book. I considered various approaches, but found none which allowed me to cover all the topics I wished to. Rather than arrange the material by chronology or geography, I have ordered the chapters in a way I hope will interest readers.

Some of the ideas in this book, and several of the places and events, have been described in articles I wrote for Taiwan's English-language newspapers or other publications. These segments have been considerably rewritten to take into account later developments, and salted more heavily with my opinions.

Throughout I have used the term "Taiwanese" to denote all islanders of Chinese descent, not only those whose ancestors arrived before the Japanese colonial era (1895-1945). For the names of people and places, I have used whichever spelling is currently the most common.

I would like to express my gratitude to the editors of those publications which have paid me to write about Taiwan for their encouragement over the past five years. I would also like to thank my friends for their stimulating comments over the years. Neither group bears any responsibility for the views expressed herein, or any errors and omissions.

KEEPING UP WITH THE WAR GOD

Motorcycle helmets, makeshift shields and fireproof clothing: We looked like ragtag riot police ready for the worst.

Just after sundown thousands of us massed in one of Yenshui's narrow streets, and encircled the scaffold frame that stood in the center of the road. Two men scurried around the structure, which was the size of a cargo container, and covered with large sheets of red paper. The technicians completed their checks, then tore off the coverings to reveal mortar-sized launch tubes and racks full of smaller rockets. The platform bristled with fireworks pointed in every direction – at the sky, at nearby houses, and, as I had been warned, at the crowd.

I heard a whistle behind me and moved quickly to one side. Stewards carved a pathway through the horde so that a wood-and-metal sedan chair could be put in position. Eight men, all dressed in the same protective fashion as the onlookers, carried it forward and set it down a few yards before the fireworks platform. This palanquin contained a colorfully attired wooden effigy the size of a large doll – a god on an inspection tour of his worldly domain. Pyrotechnicians, stewards and bearers signaled to one another. Sheaves of golden paper – currency for the god to use in the supernatural world – were scattered across the tarmac and set alight. The eight bearers then hoist the litter, and rocked it back and forth over the flames.

Most of the crowd took a few steps back. The burble of conversation died. A few seconds later the top of the frame erupted with a thunderous roar. For half a minute, the volcanic spew was of such intensity that skyward rockets created a broad, dazzling column of light. There was a brief moment of respite as the vertical fusillade waned, but then the horizontal launch tubes and racks beginning to empty themselves. People took cover behind strangers; the tall stooped. Fireworks shot like tracer bullets over my head: One glanced off my helmet's visor. The angle of fire sank lower and lower until fizzing rockets were skidding off the road surface and striking my shins.

As soon as the bombardment ended, people dispersed and searched for their friends. Strangers traded V-for-victory signs; some took off their helmets and began chatting like a cinema audience after the movie. No one wanted to lose track of the War God; soon we were following him to another part of town, where a fresh arsenal was being readied.

Yenshui is an Asian Oberammergau. Like the German village famous for its decennial Passion Play, this small Taiwanese town has little to offer outsiders other than its Plague Expulsion Parade. Tens of thousands of visitors swamp its streets and alleyways for several hours one night each February. The pandemonium dissipates at dawn, and the place returns to its usual torpor. Yenshui has been spared – or deprived of – the development which has overtaken much of Taiwan.

The Plague Expulsion Festival has an entirely different history to the Lantern Festival celebrated throughout the Chinese world on the same day. The former dates from a cholera epidemic that afflicted Yenshui almost two centuries ago.

At the height of the outbreak, the people of Yenshui carried a statue of Kuankung, the God of War, through the streets of the town. They let off firecrackers at every turn. The epidemic receded, and grateful citizens attributed the reversal to this deified soldier, who – like many other deities in the Chinese pantheon – began his existence as an ordinary human.

Tramping along Yenshui's main street, I noticed that many shop-fronts had been barricaded. Those businesses which were open enjoyed a roaring trade in edibles and cheap plastic visors. Some residents had left their cars and motorcycles parked in the road. They would regret this in the morning: Hoods and fenders suffered as people climbed atop anything which could serve as a vantage point.

The crowd swept me from the main street into a gloomy backstreet, then along a footpath beside an oily black stream. I had no idea where my friends were: Keeping up with the War God seemed much more important.

For the second onslaught I made sure that I was on the front-line. Streaks of light and starbursts filled half the sky. Helmets clashed as spectators jostled for a view of the palanquin as it heaved and sank like a small boat on a rough sea. Then, as the firepower leveled against the crowd, the people around me retreated. I found myself alone and exposed, stranded in the field of fire. Rockets enfiladed my body, but none penetrated the multiple layers of old clothing. Had I not been wearing a crash helmet, I would surely have been blinded.

The fury over, one of my friends appeared from nowhere, and thumped me several times on the shoulders and chest. I assumed he was congratulating me on having come through unscathed. Only when I took my helmet off did I realize what had caused his frenzy: The old towel that I had wrapped like a keffiyeh around my neck and shoulders was half-charred and still smoldering. The following day I heard that nearly fifty parade participants had ended up in hospital, either burned or crushed in the mayhem.

By midnight I had survived several trials-by-fireworks. Afterward I felt elated, shriven almost, and returned to Tainan aboard an overloaded taxi. The driver tried to teach the Britons, Canadians and Americans sharing his vehicle how to chant a potent Buddhist mantra which, he assured us, could prevent illnesses and mishaps.

The first Chinese New Year I spent in Taiwan was a disappointment. There were no public processions; no lion dancers; no children costumed as mythological heroes – at least not in my neighborhood. For 48 hours Tainan seemed like a ghost town. Not everyone was staying indoors, however. Many went abroad, others to mountain resorts. I had several days free and wanted to explore the island. But the queue for train tickets was forbiddingly long, so I stuck around.

Later I learned that most of the rituals connected with the Lunar New Year are conducted in private homes, hidden from sight as far as the visiting Westerner is concerned. Houses are cleaned from top to bottom. The Kitchen God is believed to ascend to Paradise and report on the behavior of each household. Before he goes, the head of each family propitiates him with candies and alcohol. On the eve of the New Year relatives gather for a feast; some kowtow to the oldest member of the household. Red envelopes are given out: Each envelope contains cash, but the money cannot be spent immediately as most shops close until the fifth day of the New Year. Fresh pictures of the Door God are pasted either side of each household's main entrance. And bad spirits are banished from the neighborhood by means of excessive noise.

This last custom was the only one to have much impact on me: For three nights running my sleep was disturbed by fire-crackers detonating at ungodly hours. (The Chinese invented gunpowder, and remind visitors of this year-round.) I felt bored and excluded during those days. But no matter: The reckless exhilaration of the Plague Expulsion Festival a fortnight later more than made up for that.

TAIPEI

Most Taiwanese aged thirty or older can remember the moment in 1975 when they heard that Chiang Kai-shek had died.

Nowadays the generalissimo's "achievements" are played down; only his enemies invoke his name. However, thousands of statues of the man remain in parks and schools around the ROC, and the Chiang Kai-shek Memorial Hall, a stone's throw from the Presidential Office, is one of Taipei's dominant landmarks.

The grounds encompass tree-shaded pathways, lawns, well-tended flowerbeds, a pond, a concert hall and a theater. Overlooking the site is the hall itself, seventy meters high and capped by blue glazed tiles which give it a vaguely Islamic look. An immense bronze statue of the late president is the centerpiece of the hall, but many visitors pay more attention to the sentries who guard it – young soldiers who stand utterly still, and who between watches must spend hours polishing their stainless steel helmets and black boots.

The museum under the hall is especially interesting, for it presents a highly orthodox version of the late president's life story. From this hagiography we learn that the Chiangs of Hsikou were of noble ancestry, and "so strict was their adherence to Confucianism that throughout the 260-year Manchu history, not a single member of the clan ever served at the alien court." This detail is included, no doubt, to underscore Chiang's belief that his successors would never compromise with the Communists who had usurped him.

The generalissimo's defeat in the civil war is mentioned

only indirectly. And nothing whatsoever is said about Mao Fu-mei, his first wife and the mother of Chiang Ching-kuo. Her name does not appear once. At the time of their arranged marriage in 1901, Miss Mao was nineteen years old; Chiang was a mere fourteen. (It was not uncommon at that time for teenage boys to marry women several years older than themselves. The girl, it was reasoned, would help raise her husband.) Mao Fu-mei was killed when Japanese planes bombed Hsikou on December 12, 1939.

A more startling omission is the generalissimo's Christianity; in this respect the Chiang Kai-Shek Memorial Hall is no different to Dr. Sun Yat-sen's mausoleum in Nanjing, where nothing – not a single crucifix – indicates that the founding father of the Republic of China was a Christian. Chiang's religion was central to his image in the Western world; but possibly the museum's organizers thought that a statement of the generalissimo's beliefs would sit oddly alongside photos of the man visiting ancestral halls, bowing before the graves of his forefathers, and engaging in other acts difficult to reconcile with Methodism. (Though they must have been aware of Chiang's religious affiliation, a group of mainland-born veterans living on Kaohsiung City's Chichin Island created a folk shrine to the generalissimo.)

Despite the unnerving historical-political symbolism of the memorial, the grounds are put to good use. All manner of events are held there: concerts, parades, political demonstrations, qi gong sessions, martial arts and disco-dancing classes. And at night, around the back of the hall, young couples behave in a manner which would have scandalized old Chiang.

*   *   *

A taxi driver who played Buddhist chants on his car stereo conveyed me to the Grand Hyatt Hotel, a five-star establishment next to the Taipei World Trade Center.

We chatted to the extent my Mandarin would allow. I asked him if he was married. He wasn't. He was too poor, he said. He didn't own the car he was driving. Perhaps I should have tipped him, but I didn't. The only Taiwanese who expect gratuities, it seems, are prostitutes, policemen and politicians.

At the hotel I introduced myself as a writer in need of information. Like most office ladies in Taipei, the desk clerk was perfectly groomed. Her face had a shiny pallor to it, a submariner's complexion.

My first question seemed to take her by surprise: "This hotel was built over a graveyard, right?"

I had been told this by a British stockbroker friend who once lived nearby with his Taiwanese wife and daughter. I had also heard that there had been a jail on this site, and that some of the political prisoners executed hereabouts had become particularly indignant spirits. Wind chimes just outside the main entrance, and calligraphy scrolls in the hotel's lobby, were carefully positioned to keep the ghosts at bay, it is said.

"Sorry, sir?" She inclined her head closer. I couldn't tell if it was to hear me better, and because this was a conversation she didn't want others to overhear.

I reworded my question. She nodded slowly and said, "I have heard that."

"Does it bother you, working above an old graveyard?" I asked.

"No."

"Not at all?"

She replied with an emphatic "No." I expressed my gratitude and left, wondering if any superstitious aunts had advised her not to work in an allegedly haunted hotel, or – more likely – had insisted that she wear an amulet to ward off the spirits of those who had been interred beneath the ground she now trod.

On an overcast morning I left my friend's apartment and walked south into Wanhua. For much of Taipei's history, Wanhua was the city's commercial heart. But the center of gravity has shifted; these days it is a blue-collar district rich in history.

My objective was Lungshan Temple, one of Taiwan's most famous places of worship. After a quick look at the inner sanctum and a circuit of its compound, I decided that Lungshan's architecture was less interesting than the people it attracted. The forecourt seemed to be populated by cripples, retardates, drunks and beggars. Inside, high school students took snapshots of each other, while worshipers – mostly middle-aged women who wore black robes over their dresses – knelt, prayed, stood up, then knelt and prayed some more.

I saw no other Westerners, even though Lungshan Temple is an attraction mentioned in English-language leaflets and marked on every tourist map. It never ceases to amaze me that droves of Europeans and North Americans visit mainland China and Japan, but bypass Taiwan. The temples of Kyoto and Nikko receive far more foreign visitors than those in Tainan, where religion seems more heartfelt. Mount Fuji is climbed by far more Westerners than Taiwan's higher and more beautiful Jade Mountain. Language is no greater an obstacle in Taiwan than in Japan. (It has to be said, however, that the Japanese authorities do use a standard romanization system for street names, and seem to have signs proofread before putting them in place: Taiwan does neither.) Japan is perceived to be a safe and orderly society, but Taiwan has never acquired a reputation for violence. Traveling around Taiwan is cheaper than visiting Japan or Hong Kong, and scarcely more expensive than the more developed parts of the mainland. Despite this – and the efforts of the Tourism Bureau – non-Asian tourists are conspicuous only by their absence.

Perhaps because I was the only foreigner around, a filthy vagabond who reeked of rice wine began following me around. I decided to move onto another temple in the neighborhood, a dank building dedicated to the god King Chingshan. Legend has it that, more than a century and a half ago, a group of fishermen carrying the king's image found themselves unable to drag it beyond this point. By throwing prognostication blocks they divined that the king wanted to stay there, so money was collected and the shrine built.

The tourist leaflet in my hands implied that this is a temple of significance, but I saw nothing I had not encountered elsewhere: statues of penny-dreadful demons with bug eyes and collar-length eyebrows; helixes of oily smoke slowly uncoiling from votive candles; altars cluttered with offerings of near-rotten fruit and wilting flowers.

Above each flight of stairs there was a list of the gods and deities which could be found on the next level. I worked my way upward, and from the fourth floor – the top – gazed out at the nearby buildings. Looking at these grimy, densely-packed blocks, it struck me then what troglodyte lives many Taiwanese lead: after work, retreating behind burglar bars into cramped dwellings where windows are closed for months on end to keep out heat, noise and dust.

Feeling claustrophobic and having inhaled suffocating quantities of incense smoke, I noticed a growing patch of blue in the sky, and decided to get out of the city. I boarded a bus heading northward over the mountains. The first stretch was an dull grind through the downtown and on past Ming Chuan University, a school named for a nineteenth-century governor remembered for his progressive policies. Liu Ming-chuan planned Taiwan's first railroad (it linked Keelung, Taipei and Hsinchu); developed the island's coal mines; established the first electricity grid in the Chinese empire; reformed the tax system; attacked corruption; and encouraged the slaughter of aborigines so Han settlers could take their land.

Then we climbed – the mountains which ring Taipei are

almost as tall as Scotland's – and passed mansions, churches and army bases before entering Yangmingshan National Park. It is the smallest of Taiwan's national parks, and certainly the most visited, but quite lovely. The road twisted between steep, grass-covered mountains. Almost too quickly for me to notice, a fumarole – a steam-belching gash big enough to swallow an apartment block – appeared on the right. Hiking trails crossed the road. I wanted to get off and explore. Then all too soon we began our descent towards the ocean. Winding down past vegetable patches and picturesque stone houses, we approached Chinshan.

Chinshan does not quite touch the coast, but nothing else about the town surprised me. Low-rise and sprawling, its neighborhoods separated by paddy fields, it has a few temples, a lively market, the usual random mix of old and new houses, plus a hillside cemetery crowded with garish graves. The air was clean and the people friendly. I liked the place immediately, but left within an hour to round the cape that is Taiwan's most northerly point.

The bus traveled within spitting distance of the surf; the greenness of the land, the rocky beach and the strong wind reminded me of Ulster. After Sanchih, whose most famous son is former President Lee Teng-hui, we approached bustling Tamsui. The bus slowed as the traffic became heavier; my escape from the city had been brief, but wonderful.

*   *   *

When I first arrived in Taiwan, I spent a few days in Taipei before heading south. While waiting for the train that would take me to Taichung, I was offered some chewing gum by a small boy. His father had encouraged him to approach me. I accepted the gum, smiled at my benefactor, and waved to his father in gratitude. The Taiwanese are truly hospitable, I said to myself.

I have never had reason to revise this opinion. Countless

times I have been asked if I needed help, if I was lost, or graciously asked which country I hailed from and why I was in Taiwan.

Unfortunately, the friendliness Taiwanese often show to Westerners is seldom extended to visitors from developing countries. I have heard Southeast Asian laborers (more than 300,000 were working in Taiwan as of mid-2001) maligned as sexual predators and troublemakers. Having grown up in homogeneous communities, many Taiwanese are acutely aware of racial dissonance. According to a survey commissioned by a Taipei City councilor in April 2000, the gathering each Sunday of hundreds of Thai and Filipino guest workers in Taipei Main Railway Station (where several businesses sell Tagalog and Thai-language videos, newspapers and books) is considered "bad" or "disgusting" by 76 percent of locals using the station; 28 percent said they "felt afraid" whenever they saw large numbers of foreigners; and 22 percent thought the Southeast Asians "would spoil the environment with litter and noise." Of course, in the nineteenth century white Americans felt much the same about Chinese immigrants.

Taiwan's media bears some responsibility for this situation. The island's newspaper editors have discovered what their counterparts elsewhere have long known: Tales of wrong-doing by foreigners go down well with local people. A good example of selective reporting was highlighted by Father Peter O'Neill writing in the *China News* in August 1998: "The faces of the six Thai workers [accused of raping a Taiwanese girl]... were sprawled across the papers... The faces of the Thai workers picking the trash from the dirty streets of Chungli [voluntary work being done to celebrate the Queen of Thailand's birthday] appeared in only one newspaper." O'Neill had invited several Chinese-language newspapers to cover the cleanup, but was dismayed by the lack of interest they showed.

Discussing such issues with friends and students was

oftentimes depressing, but always enlightening. More than one person told me, straight-faced, that racial prejudice does not exist in Taiwan. These denials seemed to be heartfelt, and probably stemmed from a combination of ignorance and wishful thinking. In fact, some of the most blatant discrimination is by Taiwanese against other Taiwanese and overseas Chinese. Language schools routinely reject applicants who look East Asian, regardless of how well they speak English. Many discos allow Westerners in for free ("foreigners' night"), and there are bars where white people pay less for beer than locals. The owners reason that where Western customers go, locals will follow. This may well be true, but at the same time there are many Taiwanese whose body language on buses, trains, in elevators and other confined places strongly suggests they are terrified of Westerners, and would go to some lengths to avoid close contact with them.

My students were surprised when I told them that if a venue in Britain offered half-price beer to Asian customers, it would be set afire within hours. And I have often wondered if the Taiwanese passion for all things Western is evidence of an open-mindedness that should be celebrated, or if it represents a grave lack of confidence in themselves, their culture and their island.

Just as archaic perceptions of homosexuality have never prompted "gay bashing," the loathing and ostracism of Southeast Asians seems not to result in racially-motivated violence. I know of only two cases where the victims were selected because of their skin color. In 1992, when Taiwan was embroiled in a trade dispute with the United States, and the US had threatened to impose limited economic sanctions, a group of young patriots in the Tainan area decided to take revenge. A South African friend was unable to refute the widespread presumption that every white person is an American, and was assaulted, though not very seriously. Around the same time, I was told that another foreigner, a Canadian, had been beaten. As far as I know, these ruffians failed to vent their anger on any US nationals.

*   *   *

Only the outrageously rich can afford a house with a garden in Taipei. But during the two-and-a-quarter years my wife and I lived there, we enjoyed the next best thing: a rooftop apartment with a view of the hills. Even better, we had the use of about twenty square meters of roof space. Yi-ju grew flowers there, and I used it for contemplative pacing while writing.

The roof area was theoretically public, but the building's other occupants almost never went there. One Sunday afternoon, however, I emerged to find my landlord and a man I'd not seen before burning ghost money. Fortunately the wind was blowing the smoke and ash away from my front door.

I asked my landlord if today was the first or the fifteenth of the lunar month: He answered that it was neither. The other man then told me they were burning the money to mark his late grandfather's birthday. As I watched the two men add more spirit money to the stainless steel furnace, I was tempted to ask if his grandfather had died of lung cancer.

*   *   *

For me, the highlight of the small northern town Sanhsia is Minchuan Street, an enchantingly traditional but sadly decrepit road. Some of the century-old houses are in a perilous state, only reinforcing girders staving off collapse. Several have already been abandoned. But under the crumbling eaves, grocers, calligraphers and coffin makers ply their trades, much as they did during the Japanese era.

Nearby stands the Tsu Shih Temple, a shrine built more than three hundred years ago in honor of Chen Chao-ying. Chen was a Sung Dynasty loyalist who refused to accept the Mongol conquest of China in the thirteenth century. He did not live to see the northern invaders driven out, but his example is said to have inspired China's people to resist their new rulers and overthrow the Mongol's Yuan Dynasty less than a century after it came to power. Not far to the south of this temple is the mausoleum of another military man who fought tenaciously, but unsuccessfully, against a change of regime in China – Generalissimo Chiang Kai-shek.

The Tsu Shih Temple has been restored several times: after earthquakes; after it was burned to the ground by Japanese soldiers in 1895 (nowhere was resistance to the Japanese takeover of Taiwan fiercer than in Sanhsia); and again after World War II. It now boasts exquisite woodwork and stone carvings. The ornate columns are rich in dragons, birds, turtles, fish, serpents, soldiers, sages, and gods.

During my 1998 visit to the temple, preparations were underway for a large-scale ceremony. A king's ransom in spirit money was stacked up in the antechambers. Row after row of red metal cans had been filled with rice; in each container a pair of scissors had been placed, along with a small circular mirror. Mystified, I took several photos which I later showed to a Taiwanese friend. She told me that the items were to be used in a ritual memorializing children who died before they could be born – those who were stillborn, miscarried or aborted.

*   *   *

One Sunday morning, quite by accident, I found the headquarters of the Lin Clansmen's Association of Taipei. The clansmen's building, which resembles a traditional shrine, is located on the roof of a modern nine-story building not far from the railway station.

Clansmen and women greeted me warmly as I wandered around the building. A banquet was being prepared; a karaoke session was in full swing. Inside were icons, hundreds of ancestor tablets, and an accouterment I had not come seen before in any place of worship – a Ping-Pong table.

*   *   *

Free enterprise has been allowed to run riot on Taiwan. Ethical and environmental considerations are often trampled underfoot. Laws and regulations do exist, but enforcement is sporadic.

Legions of unlicensed street vendors sell snacks, drinks, clothes and cheap trinkets. Personal computers are often sold with masses of pirated software thrown in for free. Some years ago, public hospitals in Chiayi noticed that an unusually high proportion of their ambulances returned empty from emergency call-outs. It emerged that private ambulance firms were eavesdropping on the calls, and sending their own vehicles to accident scenes ahead of the government ambulances. They did this to collect the bounties which some private hospitals pay for each patient brought to them.

Taiwan is a reasonably safe place to live, but its criminals are impressively sophisticated. The police have seized counterfeit silicon-chips. Numerous scams have been attempted via the Internet. The island is a world leader in credit-card fraud. And in November 2000, the public was warned that one gang was placing phony automatic-teller machines around Taipei. The fake ATMs did not dispense cash, but were a ruse to obtain the card details of those who tried to make a withdrawal.

After Chen Shui-bian was elected Taipei mayor in 1994, many of the capital's entertainment businesses (brothels, pachinko parlors, video-game arcades) were closed down, and they have not reopened. Taipei's noodle joints are cleaner than those in other cities, and the traffic is much more orderly. However, elsewhere in Taiwan – the south, and Keelung in particular – there are still neighborhoods which can be regarded as free-fire zones for entrepreneurs. In such places there is little evidence of government: Pharmacies sell prescription drugs over the counter; shops spill out onto the sidewalks; and the sex industry does little to disguise itself.

Economic freedom has resulted in severe congestion, noise and pollution, but great vitality. Compared to the UK, there are many more places to shop and eat in Taiwan, and even in Taipei prices are reasonable. A Taiwanese earning an average salary need never cook: He can afford to eat breakfast, lunch and dinner outside every day of the week.

Unemployment is still relatively low, and some sectors of the economy struggle to find workers. Rather than do low-paid work for an overbearing boss, many men and women prefer to start their own businesses. Because of strong family ties and the high savings ratio, raising capital is often easier for Taiwanese than for their counterparts in richer countries.

Taiwanese workers have fewer rights than their counter -parts in Western countries, and are often treated quite poorly by their bosses. But because of the business environment and enterprise culture, they have a much better chance of working for themselves than Britons. I now believe that the regulatory stifling of grassroots entrepreneurism in many developed countries is designed not only to protect established businesses, but also to ensure a ready supply of labor for employers.

SEX, MONEY AND POLITICS

There was a time, in the not too distant past, when Taiwan's tea houses were sedate refuges from the bustle of the world. One could relax, enjoy good conversation and partake of China's traditional beverage. But in 1997 a new breed of tea shop appeared. In such establishments neither the tea nor a particularly serene ambiance are the main attraction.

These tea houses are staffed by girls rarely older than twenty. All of them wear revealing uniforms: perilously short dresses, or camisole tops and hot pants. Taiwan's media dubbed these businesses, "spice-girl bubble tea shops." Oftentimes the tea is lousy and overpriced, but that is not important.

In some of these establishments the "spicy beauties" simply serve drinks and snacks. In others they are encouraged to chat and play cards with customers. And in a few, the "spice girls" perform erotic dances.

Such tea shops make little effort to be subtle or decorous. At one dive in Tainan, customers sit at exceptionally low tables. This forces the waitresses – whose dresses are of an eye-popping cut – to bend well forward each time they serve drinks or a snack. At another, the staff stroll up and down a catwalk, for to better show off their legs. Most Taiwanese regard these places as harmless entertainment rather than any grave affront to decency.

Betel-nut vendors use teenage girls dressed in hot pants and halter tops to hawk the nuts; spice-girl tea houses are an extension of the same logic. Given the fervid nature of free enterprise in Taiwan, it would be surprising if other businesses did not follow suit. Indeed, when a fad for Portuguese egg-tarts began to taper off, one businessman realized there was a way to boost sales. He employed some young women, outfitted them in skimpy clothes, and opened Taipei's first spice-girl egg-tart bakery. But my favorite was the betel-nut beauty I spotted while on a bus heading into Pingtung. On closer inspection the lingerie-clad temptress turned out to be a mannequin; sitting behind the dummy was a middle-aged man, ready for anyone who fell into his trap.

*   *   *

Conditions for homosexuals have changed considerably in the last few years. Gay pride marches have been held; a gay and lesbian church has been established in Taipei; the first government-registered (as opposed to underground) magazine for gays was launched in 1996.

Some Taiwanese I spoke with seemed to regard homosexuality as a primarily Western phenomenon. This ignorance and denial prevents social recognition of gay and lesbian relationships, but in some respects indirectly benefits homosexuals. I have never heard of a single instance of "gay bashing." And just as the British government declined to outlaw lesbianism because, it is said, Queen Victoria was unable to contemplate its existence, the ROC government has never bothered to restrict homosexual activity. (The communist regime on the mainland, by contrast, has imprisoned and occasionally executed homosexuals.)

Nowadays Taiwan's larger cities boast flourishing gay venues. But it seems that gay pubs and clubs seldom attract police attention. A foreign homosexual offered me a cynical explanation for this: "There's no money in it."

*   *   *

Just as some white people believe that black people are inherently better at certain sports, quite a few Taiwanese are convinced that Europeans and North Americans are incorrigibly promiscuous. Such behavior is seldom condemned; it seems to be accepted as a difference in kind between Orientals and Occidentals.

The idea that Westerners are licentious is not confined to the Far East: It is a globally pervasive notion, thanks largely to the Western films and television programs which are all most of the world's inhabitants have to go on. Some Muslim countries have become notorious for the sexual harassment which female Western tourists suffer. Taiwanese women are sometimes subjected to lewd propositioning by their male compatriots (and sometimes by Western men), but Caucasian women traveling or living in Taiwan seldom report such problems. This is because Taiwanese men – so a Canadian woman told me – find the assertiveness of the typical Western female altogether too intimidating.

The importance of remaining a virgin until marriage is instilled into many girls by their mothers, but pre-marital sex has become commonplace. Few unmarried couples openly cohabit, contraceptives are readily available and abortions are easy to arrange. But if half the stories I heard were true, the number of shotgun marriages is staggering – a phenomenon some attribute to inadequate sex education.

*   *   *

Far more Western men find Taiwanese girlfriends or wives than Taiwanese men find Western girlfriends or wives: The ratio is at least twenty to one. The situation is very similar in Japan and Singapore, I have been told.

I asked several Taiwanese women, including some who had never had a foreign boyfriend, why they thought this was. (I gave up asking Taiwanese men, finding they either attributed the fact to foreign men being "playboys," or were unwilling to express any opinion.) Some female students said they thought that women who marry Western men are likely to enjoy more freedom than those who marry their compatriots, partly because there is greater sexual equality in North America and Europe, but also because Western men are less beholden to their parents than their Taiwanese counterparts. Others cited the widespread desire to emigrate.

Few of the Western husbands I know are richer than their wives. It does seem, however, that when a Taiwanese woman marries a foreign man, that man typically comes from a richer country. But when a Taiwanese male marries a foreign female, almost always the bride is from someplace much poorer – mainland China, Vietnam, the Philippines or Indonesia. By 2001, more than 50,000 Southeast Asian women had settled down in Taiwan with their ROC husbands, and thousands of mainland brides were waiting for permission to move to the island.

                *   *   *

Taiwanese are often guilty of selfish behavior – such as littering, or leaving their cars idling unnecessarily – but it is unusual to encounter out-and-out rudeness or brusque behavior. This is one of the attractions of living in Taiwan. It is a polite and safe society. Foreigners can walk the streets without fear of racially-motivated attack or insult, and need not worry much about conventional crime.

Sometimes, however, I wished for a little less politeness and a little more consideration. Often it seemed that a lethal negligence – particularly evident on the roads – more than made up for the absence of malice. I never feared that a Taiwanese would assault or murder me. But I did worry that one might kill or maim me by accident.

*   *   *

Loan sharks and pawnshops are not the only options for Taiwanese who need to borrow money but have been turned away by the banks. The alternative – joining or forming an informal loan association – is very widespread on the island, and also used within Chinese communities in Southeast Asia, North America and Europe. These associations are known in Mandarin as hu zu hui – literally, "mutual help groups." They make unsecured loans which are neither legally enforceable nor repaid on pain of violence. The system depends on trust. The majority of hui organizers and members are women. As in Japan, managing the household's finances is considered woman's work.

A hui usually consist of a dozen to twenty people. The members are often neighbors, relatives or coworkers. If an individual does not know all the other members personally, he or she will most probably know of them. The only way to join a group is by introduction. This is not always easy to arrange: Whoever brings in an outsider puts her own reputation on the line, and stands to suffer colossal embarrassment if that newcomer later welshes on her obligations.

Each month the organizer of the hui collects funds from every member but one, and turns over all she has collected to that month's designated borrower. Every member must borrow once, but cannot borrow more than once. No money remains in the organizer's hands from month to month; the group has no assets other than a notebook in which it is recorded who has paid in, and who has borrowed. When every member has made his or her one and only withdrawal, the loan association ceases to exist. Of course, the members are free to immediately create a new circle.

Those members who have yet to collect a month's kitty pay in, say, NT$5,000 per person per month. Those who have already made their withdrawal, and are in effect repaying a loan, must deposit slightly more – perhaps NT$5,500. There are several different ways in which the sequence of withdrawals can be decided. Often an order is worked out according to the upcoming financial obligations of the members. One may have a wedding to finance in April; another may be planning to go abroad in May. Sometimes lots are drawn. In other loan associations members bid for the right to receive the following month's collection. Whichever system is used, it is always true that those who wait are well rewarded. But for those who borrow in the first few months of the hui's existence it is an expensive source of credit: Annual interest rates usually exceed 20 percent.

Hu zu hui are unregulated, unregistered and untaxed. They are certainly risky. There is no limit to the number of lending circles an individual can belong to: The temptation to join several, withdraw money from all of them in the first few months of their operating, and then disappear, must be great. In 1995, a stinky-tofu vendor in Tainan swindled nearly 200 investors and made off with over NT$100 million. I have met individuals who have lost several months' salary.

No one knows precisely what proportion of loan associations fail. When she studied rural Taiwan in the 1960s, Margery Wolf thought that collapses were "extremely rare." A quarter of a century later, Richard Hartzell estimated that one in five hui founder before completion. In addition to being less dependable than they once were (and in part for that reason), hu zu hui are declining in popularity. It is unlikely that they will die out in the near future, however, because they allow people to raise money for purposes that no bank would endorse, such as stock market speculation, or to support an obviously failing business. Some companies prohibit the organizing of hu zu hui in the workplace, fearing that if an association falls apart, staff harmony will be upset. Nevertheless, the fact that so many people do still join such groups, and that the great majority of group do survive on trust alone, is surely a reflection of certain strengths in Taiwanese society.

*   *   *

In the months following the 1995 legislative elections, hundreds of people were convicted of electoral offenses. Some were campaign workers; others were middlemen who distributed cash gifts to voters on behalf of certain candidates. But most were ordinary constituents who had sold their votes.

Many polling stations are set up inside temples. I was told that voters who accept bribes are more likely to feel bound by their promise if they must go to a place of worship to cast their ballot: Some believe the spirits enshrined there will know if they go back on their word, and punish them accordingly. This suggests that as far as Chinese gods are concerned, promises are more important than civic values.

After the Justice Ministry cracked down on vote-buying, those contesting elections were forced to devise new methods of attracting support. In elections for city mayors and county magistrates in 1997, some candidates employed skimpily-dressed female dancers and singers to perform at their rallies. And in August 1998, it was reported that certain legislative candidates were trying to win over male voters by distributing doses of the anti-impotency drug Viagra before it became legally available.

*   *   *

In few countries is the link between politics and organized crime more visible than in Taiwan.

Between 1995 and 1998, Mr. Lo Fu-chu, a non-party legislator notorious for assaulting other lawmakers, served as chairman of the legislature's judicial affairs committee, notwithstanding his reported declaration that he is the "spiritual leader" of a crime syndicate. In 2000, he was elected one of the committee's three conveners. In 2001, he was suspended for six months for assaulting a female lawmaker.

The KMT mayor of Kaohsiung and forty legislators from different political parties attended an extravagant funeral in Taipei in May 1998. They were paying their respects to Mr. Chang Chien-ho, the son of a leading figure in the Bamboo Union, one of Taiwan's largest gangs. Several other politicians, including the chairman of the DPP, sent flowers or memorial scrolls. Chang's father did not turn up. A wanted man in Taiwan, he opted to remain in mainland China.

There is a great deal of graft in local government. Much of the corruption relates to the rezoning of land for development purposes, as agricultural plots can soar in value as soon as permission to build is granted. Illegal businesses such as unlicensed KTVs, gambling arcades and brothels are often abetted by those in positions of power. Elected officials have also been known to award road-building and other contracts in return for hefty bribes. According to The Economist as much as 30 percent of all infrastructure spending is lost in kickbacks.

In 1995, a former mayor of Taichung was jailed for his role in a land scandal, and the chief of Pingtung County, Mr. Wu Tze-yuan, was sentenced to life imprisonment on corruption charges in 1996. Later the same year prosecutors sought to jail Wu's counterpart in Taoyuan County for his involvement in a land appropriation scandal. They were unsuccessful: before the judicial process could be completed, Mr. Liu Pang-yu was shot dead, along with seven other people who happened to be in his home at the time. Many are convinced that the massacre was the work of gangsters who had failed to dissuade the county chief from demolishing illegal entertainment establishments they were running. It is by no means certain that Liu would have been imprisoned even if he had been found guilty: Six years after his conviction, Wu Tze-yuan had still not served a single day of his sentence. While free on "medical parole," Wu ran as a non-party candidate in the 1998 elections and won a seat in the legislature. A few months after those elections, another lawmaker, Mr. Chen

Chao-ming, received a jail term of eight years for rigging public-works bids.

In local politics, the positions of council speaker and deputy speaker are pivotal. When electing colleagues to these posts, some council members have sold their votes. In 1998, a former deputy speaker of Kaohsiung County, Mr. Huang Chen -kuai, was sentenced to 26 months in jail after bribing his way to victory. He had reportedly spent in excess of NT$14 million. One of his coconspirators, Mr. Wu Ho-sung, became speaker at the same time but was never brought to trial: Not long after his election he was shot dead, ironically while attending a funeral. The crime of former Pingtung County Council Speaker Mr. Cheng Tai-chi was altogether more serious: He murdered a local businessman who had refused to pay protection money for a casino he operated in the speaker's constituency. Cheng was executed in August 2000.

Funds disbursed to local governments to help them rebuild after the September 21 earthquake of 1999 provided fresh opportunities for corruption. One Nantou County township leader received a life sentence in June 2001, and the county's chief, Pang Pai-hsien, was arrested.

*   *   *

For decades the Nationalists suppressed Hokkien, the Taiwanese language. Students were punished if they spoke it in school; television broadcasts in the dialect were limited; traditional puppet shows were outlawed. Now, however, the vernacular is de rigueur. Entertainers and politicians routinely speak it; some job advertisements specify that applicants must be fluent in the dialect.

An air force officer – a staunch unificationist who apparently feared the political implications of the island having its own language – told me there was no such thing as

"Taiwanese," and the dialect should be called *Min-nan-hua*, "the language spoken south of the River Min." The Min flows through Fujian province. The region south of it is where a great many of the Chinese who migrated to Taiwan in the seventeenth, eighteenth and nineteenth centuries came from. Calling the vernacular *Min-nan-hua* was, for this man, a way of stressing the islanders' ancestral links to the mainland.

*　　　*　　　*

Another air force officer invited me to the dismal apartment he shared with his wife. After dinner, he complained bitterly about the cantonment accommodation assigned to professional soldiers. Many barracks and married quarters are shoddy structures dating from the 1950s, built cheaply on the assumption they would not be needed for long, he said. During that era, the Nationalists told everyone that Taiwan was only their temporary home, and that they would recover the mainland within a few years.

*　　　*　　　*

Taiwan has a number of *pai-fangs*, commemorative stone arches. One of the most exquisite is in the center of Kincheng, a town on the island of Kinmen.

An information panel in Chinese and passable English describes the arch's background. It was erected in 1812 in honor of the mother of a onetime provincial governor. The lady forswore remarriage during her 28 years of widowhood; her loyalty to her late husband was considered exemplary.

The arch itself is a superb piece of work, both imposing and attractive. The information panel looks fine, but on closer inspection turns out to have been made of plastic. It is supported by fiberglass panels dressed up to resemble stone. That such materials were used seems very odd. There are several collapsed old houses in the neighborhood: Any one of them would have provided more than enough granite for a more lasting and weatherproof installation. Unfortunately, a slapdash attitude to relics is all too common on the part of the authorities.

*   *   *

During English classes I did not avoid politics, but I always found current issues less interesting than the ways in which Taiwan's peculiar history has touched people's lives.

I met individuals whose relatives had been victims of the February 28 Incident in 1947, when discontent with the KMT regime led to riots and massacres which cost thousands of lives. One young lady recalled as a child seeing her church minister (a political activist) arrested in mid-service. And a graduate student told me that in the late 1970s, his cousin – then a pupil at a prestigious high school in central Taiwan – was arrested for scrawling a pro-independence slogan on a blackboard.

The boy's parents lobbied for his release, and the next day he was freed without charge. In due course he completed his schooling, graduated from university, and did his military service. Like many other bright young men and women, he aspired to become a civil servant. He sat the examination several times, but failed every time. Meanwhile, some of his less able acquaintances were successful. He eventually realized that, because of his impulsive act years earlier, his name was probably on a blacklist. Reckoning he had no prospects in the public sector, he became a businessman.

*   *   *

When tutoring teenagers and young adults one-to-one, I often found myself playing the role of agony aunt. Students would discuss subjects they dared not broach with their family or school teachers: Some confessed to having a lover their relatives would never accept, or to having cheated in a major exam. Several college-bound students bemoaned being directed by their parents to select majors they had no interest in. They dared not defy the advice for fear of being considered ungrateful.

There were also quiet individuals who turned out to be full of paranoia, invective, venom and even hatred. They would spend entire classes fulminating against their enemies – real or imagined, I often could not tell.

But one of the pleasures was that sometimes the most ordinary students would give fascinating responses to common questions.

On one occasion I asked a large class of nineteen- and twenty-year-olds in which foreign country they would most like to live. The top three choices were, predictably, the USA, Canada and Japan. One girl, however, nominated Libya.

I thought maybe I had misheard her, but she confirmed that, given the choice, she would live in the North African country. When I asked why, she told me that her father had been living there for several years, and was involved in the import-export business.

Later I realized that I should have asked her how her father could do international trade from Libya, as at that time the country faced United Nations economic sanctions. She would probably have pointed out that Taiwan is not a member of the UN.

*   *   *

Many of the high-school students I taught complained they were under tremendous pressure to do well. But the grisliest tale of parental expectations – and disappointment – was told by a young woman living and working in Tainan County:

"For a time, one of my uncles wanted to move my grandfather's grave. He believed the grave's position had brought him bad luck, and was the reason why his only son has never returned home.

"But I think there's another reason why my cousin never goes home. The first time he took the university entrance examination, he failed badly. My uncle was so angry and disappointed he decided to teach my cousin a lesson. Using a pair of scissors, he cut off part of one of my cousin's ears.

"My cousin tested into a college in north Taiwan the following year, and he now works in Taipei. He's not returned to his hometown for several years, and never contacts his father."

*   *   *

A British friend was locked up for twelve days. He was denied natural light and fresh air, and forbidden from writing letters, making phone calls or even receiving them. Moreover, he had to work hard.

This incarceration was voluntary and quite lucrative. My friend worked as an English lecturer at a college, and had been asked to help prepare one of that summer's entrance examinations. With other teachers, some typists and a couple of janitors, he was taken to a school dormitory which had been cleared and sealed off for the occasion. Inside, he and two colleagues wrote the English-language segment of the test, plus additional questions for a backup version should the original be compromised. All the notes from their brainstorming sessions were shredded; the students brought in to try out a provisional version of the test were also sequestered. The test papers were printed in the dormitory. Once their work had been done, the writing teams, the printers and the others were free to do whatever they wished – so long as they stayed in the building and did not attempt to communicate with the outside world until the real examination concluded a week later.

*   *   *

Television newscasts routinely show emergency-room personnel battling to resuscitate accident victims, and intrusive shots of relatives almost unhinged by grief. When the teenage daughter of a famous TV personality was kidnapped and murdered in 1997, pictures of the girl's battered corpse were shown on television and in newspaper reports. After a China Airlines jet crashed near Taipei in February 1998, live broadcasts from the site included close-ups of dismembered bodies. When rioters in Indonesia raped and murdered several ethnic Chinese, Taiwanese magazines did not hesitate to print gruesome photos of the victims' injuries. (By contrast, atrocities against the inhabitants of East Timor received little coverage.)

It is not unusual for media personnel to impede rescue workers. McGill Alexander, a South African diplomat wounded in a shoot-out between police and Taiwan's most-wanted criminal, experienced this firsthand when medical attendants were unable to move him and his seriously-wounded daughter to waiting ambulances because of the selfish zeal of local reporters and camera crews. In his book *Hostage in Taipei*, he likens the media to African wild dogs who "tear chunks of flesh from their victim… [and] will literally eat [it] alive."

Had I not felt the great kindness of many locals, and witnessed the impressive outpouring of concern and generosity that followed the September 21 earthquake of 1999, the local media would by now have convinced me that the Taiwanese are a ghoulish people fascinated by death and disaster, with little regard for human dignity or life.

*   *   *

The Republic of China is hemorrhaging talent. Each year tens of thousands of its brightest and richest citizens emigrate. The most popular destinations are the United States, Canada, Australia and New Zealand. Significant numbers have moved to South Africa, Brazil, Argentina, Belize and other places. There has long been a sizable Taiwanese community in Japan.

I met dozens of people who aimed to leave for good. Most had cogent reasons for wanting to go, but in some cases I sensed the person was motivated by an *idee fixe* that life in the West is, and always will be, better than life in Taiwan. One government official, talking about his parents, alluded to this: "For my mother, living in the US is a prestige issue."

Sometimes I suggested alternative courses of action. Relocating to Taiwan's environmentally-attractive east coast is far cheaper – and obviously involves much less cultural adjustment – than moving to a different continent. I even suggested that would-be emigrants try to improve conditions in Taiwan, rather than join the *sauve qui peut*. However, in the course of teaching teenagers and adults from a variety of backgrounds, I came across an unsettling number of people who, when certain social or environmental problems were being discussed, denied there was anything they could do to change the situation. Instead of "If we all do a little, together we can do a lot," again and again I heard: "I'm only one person. What can I do?" (Michael Hsiao (Hsiao Hsin-huang), perhaps Taiwan's most famous sociologist, and Lester Milbrath write that while many people regard pollution as a problem, they do not see it as "requiring correction by their individual action.")

This would be called hopelessness, were it accompanied by despair rather than apathy. Some attribute it to Taiwan's authoritarian past, others to age-old Chinese notions of quietism. Whatever the cause, social reforms should not be beyond a people who have created an economic miracle, and whose political progress has been exemplary.

TREATY PORTS

I had an urge to visit Keelung, because it has been the site of some notable contacts between China and the West.

The Spanish set up a trading post there in 1626: They called it La Sanctissima Trinidad. Sixteen years later they were forced out by the Dutch, whose bases in south Taiwan were flourishing. The latter chose an excellent moment to attack: The Spanish, distracted by an uprising in the Philippines, had withdrawn most of their garrison. A plague outbreak had weakened the remaining forces. After six days of fighting the Spanish capitulated. In 1662 the Dutch were thrown out by Ming Dynasty loyalists fleeing mainland China; they retook the port a year later, but quit for good in 1668.

During the First Opium War Keelung was the scene of heavy fighting. The British tried to capture the harbor three times. In the course of the first assault in August 1841, several British vessels were sunk and hundreds of sailors taken prisoner. The second and third attacks were also beaten back. (This is not taught in British schools.) But the pugnacity of Keelung's defenders made no difference to the outcome of the war: The imperial court in Peking sued for peace in 1842, and ceded Hong Kong Island to Great Britain.

An opportunity for revenge soon presented itself. Two British vessels were shipwrecked off the northern coast a few months after the war's end: 197 survivors were summarily executed. British diplomats protested vigorously, but no doubt remembering the bloody nose they had recently been given, took no punitive action.

Keelung became a treaty port in 1863. Large quantities of coal, camphor and tea were exported. But peace did not last, and during the course of an obscure Sino-French conflict in 1884-85, French marines occupied the city and wantonly pulled down the fortress which had seen off the British four decades earlier.

History is not Keelung's only draw. I had been told that one of the temples in the area has a specialist role: Prostitutes and brothel-keepers go there and pray for good business. I had a prurient desire to see this place, but unfortunately no one was able to tell me either the address of the temple or its name. I would have felt a fool, traipsing around an unfamiliar city, asking passers-by if they knew where the prostitutes' temple was. So instead of spending a day in Keelung, I traveled to Tamsui.

*   *   *

Tamsui means "freshwater," yet like many other waterways on the west coast, the Tamsui River has suffered the consequences of the island's rapid industrialization. While it does not literally curdle like some Taiwanese streams, it is far from healthy. Despite this, Tamsui town is a pleasant and interesting place. Like Keelung it used to be a treaty port. But these days it has a less commercial mien.

A few years after establishing themselves in Keelung, the Spanish extended their influence to Tamsui. Here they built a citadel which still stands; it ranks amongst the oldest buildings in Taiwan. The Spanish named it Fort Santo Domingo, but in local parlance it has long been known as *hung-mao-cheng*, "the fort of the red-haired barbarians." British diplomats occupied Fort San Domingo for more than a century; during that time they did not pay a penny in rent. But a legacy of that era, the elegant redbrick residence built for the consul in 1891, perhaps makes up for some of these arrears.

Within the ex-consulate are cells where British nationals were detained. Foreign traders, like their counterparts in Shanghai, enjoyed extraordinary rights, but were subject to the jurisdiction of their home countries. In both Taiwan and mainland China, the humiliation of extraterritoriality is remembered and talked about, even now. The reasons why Western nations demanded this privilege for their citizens – the venality of Chinese judges and the widespread use of torture to extract confessions – are not. (Similar terms imposed on Japan in the 1860s inspired the Meiji authorities to reform their legal system.)

The British mission pulled out in 1972, midway through the exodus of embassies which humiliated Chiang Kai-shek and his regime. Perhaps the oddest victims of the resulting diplomatic isolation have been the 81 dead foreigners who lie buried in an old cemetery not far from Tamsui Oxford College (a Christian school unconnected to Britain's Oxford University). Sometime in the late nineteenth century, Tamsui's foreign residents appropriated a piece of land to be their graveyard. The exact date is unknown, because no title deed existed until 1909. Only then did the Japanese colonial authorities – sticklers for proper documentation – assign formal possession of the lot to the British Consulate. The British took care of the cemetery until they broke off relations with the ROC. The Australian legation then assumed responsibility. They in turn left, and turned over control of the plot to the American Embassy.

When Taiwan's most important ally recognized Beijing in 1978, the land became ownerless and neglected. Local residents used it as a rubbish dump, and several tombstones were removed for use in construction work elsewhere. Finally a group of Canadian expatriates decided to renovate the graveyard. Their annual clean-up exercise coincides with Chingming Festival, the traditional springtime tomb-sweeping holiday.

Finding the cemetery is not as easy as it should be. There are no signs to it in the neighborhood. It has yet to become a tourist attraction like the much larger foreigners' graveyard in Yokohama. The first time I went there, I was dismayed to find the only gate padlocked, and the walls too high to climb. But what I could see inside inspired me to persist. After a quick glance in every direction I clambered over the gate and splashed down in the mud on the other side.

The plot is not much larger than a tennis court, and gloomy on account of overhanging trees. A swarm of mosquitoes greeted me; I wondered how many of those buried here had died of malaria or dengue fever. The tombstones are uniformly gray -brown, but the inscriptions vary greatly in legibility. One of the clearest reads:

TO THE GLORY OF GOD AND THE BELOVED MEMORY OF ADRIAN CONWAY EVANS, HBM VICE CONSUL IN FORMOSA, BORN JUNE 14TH 1905. DROWNED WHILE BATHING AUGUST 15TH 1952 TOGETHER WITH HIS FRIEND OSMOND SMYTH WHO GAVE HIS OWN LIFE IN TRYING TO SAVE HIM.

The more recent graves are the easiest to decipher: the unnamed daughter of a US Army captain, died May 8, 1956; a two-month-old infant buried in 1966; and what seems to be the final interment: the tomb of a missionary who died in 1974. More than a quarter of those buried here died before reaching the age of twelve. Until well after World War II, Taiwan was a pestilential place whose fevers and maladies struck infants hardest.

Fifteen Britons, nineteen Americans and a dozen Canadians lie in the foreigners' cemetery. With them are more than two dozen individuals whose names and nationalities are not known. Most are souls who drowned off the coast of Taiwan. Washed ashore and stripped naked by beachcombers, they would have been handed over to the foreign community for an austere Christian disposal. Many headstones state the deceased's erstwhile occupation, with the graves of Mammon's representatives slightly outnumbering God's. The life expectancy of the tea tasters, traders and shipping agents in old Formosa was not at all good. In addition to deaths which could be attributed to the unhealthy environment, some caught syphilis from prostitutes, or became opium addicts.

Tamsui's most famous Western resident does not repose in the foreigners' cemetery. Dr. George Leslie Mackay and his descendants have been accorded a separate graveyard. Mackay, a Presbyterian missionary from Canada who arrived in Tamsui in 1872 and died there in 1901, is celebrated as the founder of churches, schools, a hospital, and Tamsui Oxford College (now Aletheia University). Almost uniquely among missionaries of his era, he took a Chinese wife; their only son became a church minister and educator in Tamsui.

While on furlough in Canada in 1896, Mackay authored an account of his experiences. Only a supremely self-confident Victorian, unconstrained by political correctness or cultural relativism, could have written *From Far Formosa*. In it the missionary sums up religious life on the island, concluding that: "[The] heathenism of Formosa is of the same kind and quality as the heathenism of China. It is the same poisonous mixture, the same dark, damning nightmare." He condemns Taoism as, "a system of demonolatry." And he recounts building one church in a way calculated to confound those who believe in geomancy "to show the heathen that their notion of good luck was vain superstition."

Mackay's book also belies a notion some more recent foreign residents have had – that before industrialization the island was an agrarian Shangri-La. The missionary survived earthquakes, typhoons, wars, xenophobic mobs and epidemics. On one occasion he almost died of meningitis. On another he returned home to find a two-meter-long serpent in his living room.

The custom of foot-binding appalled Mackay, as did the

dishonesty of local bureaucrats. Some of the people he ministered to believed malaria could be contracted by treading on sheets of ghost money. Although he was not a qualified physician, the medical work he did made him many friends. He extracted 21,000 teeth, conveyer-belt fashion, and returned every one to its owner so as to avoid arousing suspicions that he was a sorcerer. Butter, milk and cheese were unavailable on the island. Tamsui was, "a smoky, dirty town." Nowhere in his book does Mackay describe the Taiwanese people as frugal or industrious. But while walking from one rural mission to the next, he sometimes saw scaly anteaters and tiger-cats – animals now extremely rare or extinct. And, of course, he never encountered a traffic jam.

DEAD PRESIDENTS

Some people in the PRC maintain that after Chiang Kai-shek died in 1975, his remains were transported secretly to the mainland and interred near his ancestral home in Zhejiang province. But no Taiwanese person I have spoken to believes that such a thing could have happened. Given the state of cross-strait relations at that time, it does seem extremely unlikely.

Another equally improbable rumor heard exclusively on the mainland alleges that before the Kuomintang retreated to Taiwan, they opened up the mausoleum of Dr. Sun Yat-sen in Nanjing and removed his body to Taipei. This story persists, despite it being well known that the KMT ruled out moving Sun's remains in 1937, when Japanese troops were poised to seize the city. They abandoned their attempts to open the mausoleum then because it had been so robustly constructed that only explosives could have done the job. Still, some people seem to be convinced that shuffling dead leaders from one part of China to another is skulduggery typical of the dastardly Nationalists.

Officially, Chiang Kai-shek and his son, Chiang Ching-kuo, lie in "temporary repose" beside Lake Compassion, about 45 kilometers south of Taipei. The gentle hills, bamboo groves and acacia trees supposedly reminded the elder Chiang of his Zhejiang hometown.

Both bodies rest above ground: the generalissimo's in a villa that he used as a retreat; his son's in a near-identical building a few kilometers away. Both men stipulated that they should be buried only when China is reunified and governed according to

Sun's Three Principles, but some are saying that it is time the two presidents were given a proper, permanent burial.

(Yen Chia-kan, who served as the ROC's head of state between Chiang Kai-shek's death and the accession of Chiang Ching-kuo in 1978, did not follow the precedent set by the Chiangs, and was buried in Taipei's National Military Cemetery.)

In the three years following the death of Chiang Kai-shek, two million people traveled to Lake Compassion to pay their respects. For a time only officially-approved groups could enter the site. Later, visitors had to show their ID cards or passports before entering the grounds. But by the time Yi-ju and I visited on a sweltering summer's day in 2000, these requirements had been dropped. Sightseers can appear unannounced, walk past the military policemen who guard the villa, and, under the watchful eyes of a young official, spend a few moments regarding the late president's black marble sarcophagus.

What with the sunlight streaming in, casually dressed families sauntering through, and a portrait of Chiang smiling on the wall, the setting was far from funereal. The lotus emblems decorating the base of the sarcophagus intrigued me: these flowers are associated with Buddhism. The only indication of the generalissimo's Christian faith was a floral crucifix placed before his coffin on behalf of Madame Chiang.

A twisting walkway links the elder Chiang's mausoleum with that of his son. Nowadays hardly anyone uses the path, and it is not well maintained. Chiang Ching-kuo gets few visitors, despite having been, in popular estimation, a far better president than his father.

The younger Chiang, a ruthless secret policeman in the 1940s and 1950s, evolved into an approachable and capable politician. He mingled with ordinary folk much more often than his father. Whenever he toured a place, it was his habit to exchange hats with one of the locals. But while countless statues, mountains, roads, and schools recall the generalissimo, there are few physical reminders of Chiang Ching-kuo.

The younger Chiang fathered five sons, three by his Russian-born wife, two by a Chinese mistress during World War II. The only survivor of the five is John Chang, an ex-diplomat who has served as foreign minister, vice premier and KMT secretary-general. Chang has always used his mother's family name; his paternity was not made public until after his father had passed away. His twin brother, an academic, and his three half-brothers all died in their late forties or early fifties. Experts in geomancy ascribe these untimely deaths to one fact: The bodies of the men's father and grandfather still lie above ground. Throughout the Chinese world, proper disposal of the deceased is considered crucial. Failure to formally bury a dead person may bring great misfortune to a family.

It is not known if the Chiangs weighed the possibility that their stance would imperil their descendants. Chiang Kai-shek, despite his Christianity, certainly had some regard for the precepts of geomancy. In 1927, he sent a special military unit to Mao Zedong's hometown with orders to desecrate the graves of the Communist leader's ancestors. If this was done, Chiang apparently believed, disaster upon disaster would befall Mao. The mission failed because a peasant led the soldiers to a different set of graves, those of a landlord's family who happened to have the same surname. (Even Mao, despite his campaigns against old ideas, seems to have reckoned fengshui to be something more than mere superstition. After deposing Liu Shaoqi at the beginning of the Cultural Revolution, he ordered the razing of Liu's ancestral home – a move intended to forestall any recovery in his rival's fortunes.)

If a corpse is to be properly dealt with, it must be buried, not cremated. This seems strange in light of other traditional practices. Burning does not imply disrespect: It is the usual method of sending items to the afterworld. Ghost money must be burned if it is to be of use to one's ancestors. At funerals, things intended for the deceased – paper cars and intricate model houses – are always dispatched in this manner. This latter custom is still very common in Taiwan. But there is a powerful reason why, even now, some people cannot accept any alternative to burial. Traditionally, the Chinese have believed that any form of mutilation renders a body unfit to receive a soul again and be resurrected. (In the case of some emperors, this notion went so far as to cause all the hair, teeth and parings of the nails that had been shed in life to be placed with the corpse in the coffin.)

This desire to be buried whole has also caused a general aversion to amputation: A limb hanging uselessly is sometimes preferred to a prosthesis. And in previous centuries, condemned criminals almost always opted for painfully slow strangulation rather than instantaneous decapitation.

Allowing your body to be mutilated before or after death not only jeopardizes your prospects of rebirth: It is also disrespectful to your parents. According to the *Classic of Filial Piety*, "Our body and limbs, our hair and skin are given us by our parents, and we must be careful not to injure them: this is the beginning of filial piety." Such beliefs have long hampered medicine in the Chinese world: Transplantable organs are always in short supply, and medical students lack cadavers on which to practice. Taiwanese hospitals use to waive the treatment fees of dead, indigent patients if their relatives consented to the removal of suitable organs. Now that the government has introduced a universal health insurance system, this source of organs has dried up.

Some Taiwanese still subscribe to these traditional ideas, among them the parents of a Kaohsiung councilwoman who died after a bungled kidnapping on the mainland in 1998. They objected to the PRC authorities carrying out an autopsy on their daughter, and believing that the deceased's spirit had to be summoned home before there could be a funeral, they arranged for two Taoist priests to perform rites at the hospital where their daughter had died.

Changes of regime in China have sometimes been followed by the exhumation and dismemberment of the previous rulers. More than a century ago, sinologist J.J.M. de Groot wrote: "[As] mutilation prevents a body from ever reviving, then destroying the remains of an enemy is the most refined means of revenge."

In 1928, soldiers allied to Chiang Kai-shek opened the tomb of the Dowager Empress Tzu Hsi and hacked her body to pieces. The same fate is unlikely to befall the two late presidents so long as they remain in Taiwan, but some members of the Chiang clan support sending the remains back to Zhejiang for burial there. Others would be satisfied if the men were properly interred in Taiwan. Either solution could be construed as a surrender of sorts. There has been no movement on the issue for years.

JADE MOUNTAIN

"Hello! Welcome to Taiwan! Where do you come from?"

Eric had disappeared on a mission to procure hot coffee, leaving me at Chiayi's bus station to mind our backpacks and deal with an overgregarious English-speaker. The man, in his fifties, had traveled down from Taipei the previous night. He worked for the government's agriculture department, and was heading to a pig auction on the outskirts of the city. His zeal at six o'clock in the morning was impressive: "I have to find out why pork is so cheap now. We think some of the wholesalers are importing meat illegally from the mainland. I have to persuade them to stop doing this. It's bad for Taiwanese farmers, and the meat may not be safe to eat."

I was in no mood for a conversation; I smiled at the man and hoped his bus would come soon. The smuggling of pork into Taiwan did not surprise me: Almost every day the newspapers report interceptions, seizures and arrests. Among the goods illicitly shipped in from the mainland are tea, mushrooms, herbal medicine, seafood, garlic, cigarettes, and delicacies such as chickens' testicles, ducks' tongues and cows' bladders. There is a constant flow of illegal immigrants (some of whom have been exposed by their inability to sing the Republic of China's national anthem), firearms and drugs. Taiwanese gangs have set up laboratories in Fujian to manufacture amphetamines; ROC nationals have been executed by the Communist authorities for drugs offenses. There is some reciprocity in the smuggling. Vehicles are stolen in Taiwan and resold in the Communist state.

It is said that one Taiwanese businessman stumbled across his car in a mainland parking lot some months after it had been stolen from a Taipei street. Scores of fugitives from ROC justice are believed to be hiding out on the mainland.

The government worker's monologue did not abate. When Eric returned I abandoned the two of them, and went for a stroll. Chiayi struck me as thoroughly dismal that morning. For me, the city will never be anything more than a place I need to pass through on the way to somewhere far more inspiring: Yushan (Jade Mountain) National Park. Taiwan's premier nature reserve, it is a haven for wildlife, and encompasses wooded uplands, unspoiled valleys and the island's highest peak.

"Did that guy say anything interesting to you?" I asked Eric as we took our seats on the seven o'clock bus to Alishan.

"Yeah, he invited me to visit him and his family in Taipei. He's got three unmarried daughters, but he warned me that none of them are beautiful."

The traditional way of reaching Alishan is by train. A narrow-gauge railway, built by the Japanese in 1912, links the resort to the lowlands. But the track was not laid with tourists in mind: The colonial regime underwrote its construction because they wanted to exploit the cedar and cypress forests in the area. For decades logging camps dotted the hillsides around Alishan. Reforestation is now the order of the day, but an illicit lumber industry still exists. Local men have been jailed for rustling camphor trees out of the forest and into clandestine sawmills.

When the train is running (often it is not), it is twice as ex-pensive as the bus, and only half as fast. Yet on public holidays tickets often sell out. In East Asia no railroad can compare to the Alishan Forestry Railway: Over the course of 75 kilometers it passes through fifty tunnels and over 77 bridges. Complete loops have been built to overcome the steepest sections. Passengers ascend through broad-leaf forest, bamboo groves and mixed forest, before reaching an altitude at which conifers flourish. There is no better way to see the marvelous range of tree species Taiwan has been endowed with, and no more scenic route to Alishan. But for Eric and I, time was the most important consideration.

Taiwan's plains have been ravaged by heavy industry, but the island's mountainous interior remains largely pristine. On the highway between Chiayi and Alishan one particular village straddles these two realms. A grim cement factory sullies its seaward side, but inland of the settlement perennially green highlands rise upward, giving heart to those who are weary of the cities.

The bus wheezed and slowed as it tackled the gradient. Soon we were in prime betel-nut-growing country. The trees resemble small tropical palms, and grow well up to an altitude of about a thousand meters – thereafter tea becomes the main crop. Farmers refer to betel-nut as "green gold": acre for acre it is the most lucrative thing that can be grown. It is also one of the most beautiful: A hillside bristling with these straight-trunked trees is a delight to gaze upon. But betel-nut monoculture has increased soil erosion and the frequency of landslides. The tree's roots are shallow, its leaves too small to shade the topsoil and retain much moisture.

Only on those slopes too steep to cultivate has nature been allowed to take its course. Bushes tangle with ferns. The variety of greens is astonishing: Every imaginable hue fights for preeminence. The only places where bare rock and soil are visible are those where recent landslides have degloved the surface.

The bus paused for breath at Shihco. South of us, but invisible due to the mountain fog, were villages belonging to the Tsou aboriginal tribe. A few miles to the north of Shihco lies Fenchihu, a village which prospers from tea, tourism and horticulture. Once I had stayed overnight in Fenchihu, and met the resident Catholic missionary, an impressively multilingual

European. Able to compress a decade of living in the mountains into a single afternoon of conversation, he told me that prior to the lifting of martial law, he once inadvertently rented out his church hall to a group of political dissidents who wanted to hold a secret meeting.

Alishan is regarded as one of the most beautiful places in Taiwan. The reputation is undeserved: I think of it as a car park surrounded by hotels and overpriced restaurants. The resort began as a Japanese hill station, a retreat from the hot plains, much like Darjeeling was for the British in India. There is an adjacent aboriginal settlement, but few visitors set foot there.

On previous excursions I had done everything there was to do in Alishan. I had lingered beside Two Sisters Pond, admired the 3,000-year-old Sacred Tree (since been cut down for safety reasons) and waited with hundreds of others atop Celebration Mountain for the sun to rise. It is an interesting place to observe the forms and conventions of Taiwanese tourism – pathological feasting, group photographs, guides who use megaphones to communicate their fervor. But I felt no desire to spend time there again. When the bus pulled up outside the archway which marks the entrance to the resort, Eric and I got off, and began walking in the opposite direction.

The air at 2,200 meters was cool, damp and invigorating. I shook off the stupor I had sunk into on the bus, and rediscovered my relish for what promised to be a exciting expedition. This sense of anticipation did not last, however. The first ride we got took us only as far as Tzuchung, a tiny settlement – a few farmers and a police outpost – not much beyond Alishan. It was raining by the time we got there. Eric and I discussed the weather nervously; the previous evening he had warned me that two typhoons were forecast to hit Taiwan in the next few days. We had laughed about it, and decided to go ahead with our trek. But things were not looking so good now.

As we stood in the drizzle waiting for onward transport, a policeman emerged from the station. He was stocky, brown-skinned and exceptionally friendly – a Bunun aborigine. Honesty about our plans could have prompted demands to see mountain permits, so we told him that we were merely hitch-hiking along the highway. He seemed happy with that, and helped us flag down a car. Once aboard we asked the driver to drop us off at Tatachia, where we would begin walking; he accepted this countermanding of the policeman's instruction without question. Minutes later we were inside the National park. After rounding several bends, we arrived at Tatachia, a saddle area from where – had it been a clear day – we could have looked up and seen Jade Mountain.

We heaved our packs out of the car boot, thanked the driver, and set off without much enthusiasm. The sun was behind the clouds, and it was getting downright cold. We trudged up a surfaced side road before coming to the trailhead. The amenities there amounted to some refuse bins and a signboard. We did not so much as glance at the latter: The path to White Cloud Hostel, Jade Mountain's base camp, was one both Eric and I had trodden several times before.

It is said that when the Japanese conducted the first comprehensive topographical survey of Taiwan, they were grievously upset to find the island had at least three mountains higher than their own Fuji. They overestimated Jade Mountain's height somewhat, but determined correctly that it is the tallest point on the island. Bestowing a Japanese name on the mountain, they gazetted the peak as "Niitakayama, the highest peak in the Empire." It is now reckoned to be 3,952 meters (12,966 feet) high.

We walked until the middle of the afternoon, ascending

gently on a well-worn. There were few trees on the hillside, just thick grasses, thistles and wildflowers. Rounding a corner a few kilometers from White Cloud Hostel, Eric and I were granted our first proper view of Jade Mountain itself. It is an impressive massif – a rock pyramid whose top half is bereft of vegetation. A few times each year, usually in January or February, the summit receives a topping of snow. But heavy falls are rare: South Taiwan's winters are usually dry, and the peak is barely north of the Tropic of Cancer.

A gale of elemental strength ruled out camping. We retreated ignominiously, and ended up pitching our tent barely three kilometers from the trailhead. Our day's progress could only be described as pitiful. We consoled ourselves with a bottle of wine.

The next morning our friends caught up with us before we broke camp. Lief smiled; Richard, who had expected us to be much, much further up the trail, greeted us with a bellow of dismay: "What the hell are you doing here?"

It drizzled steadily throughout the morning; visibility was poor. I had read that philosophers in the China of yore believed mountain mists to possess revitalizing properties. But as the four of us trudged onward and upward I simply felt cold and miserable. We mustered and cooked dinner at White Cloud Hostel. Scores of Taiwanese hikers were already lodged there. Lief and Eric opted to outrun the crowd and camp on the summit itself, five hundred meters higher up. Richard and I pitched our tent amidst a dozen others. We went to sleep beneath a glorious array of stars, surrounded by sounds of camaraderie.

At 3:30 a.m. we boiled water for coffee, made porridge, and dismantled the tent. The temperature was around zero, the air still and the sky mostly clear. People stumbled around the encampment, steaming metal mugs in their hands. No one said much: Holiday spirit had given way to a mood of grim determination.

Between White Cloud Hostel and the summit the trail consists of steep, repetitive switchbacks. After half an hour of steady tramping we were out of the forest. Our flashlights were unnecessary: We could make out the route by moonlight. A party of hikers, eager to reach the summit before sunrise, passed by as I squatted beside the trail, resting for a few minutes. I offered some cheery encouragement: The walkers responded breathlessly, and shuffled onward as joylessly as pallbearers.

Beyond the highest of the gorse and brambles, we reached a point where there was no discernible path. A tumble of boulders lay between us and the next stretch of trail. We knew from experience that the chain slung across it was essential to further progress up the mountain. I pulled myself up from one ledge to the next. Through my thin gloves the metal links felt like chunks of ice. Struggling uphill fully-laden, I was painfully conscious of the thinness of the air. My chest heaved; moisture deserted my mouth each time I gasped for breath.

A hundred meters or so shy of the summit, we set our packs down and waited for Lief and Eric. I was glad to forgo the final stretch: It consists of more chains, bleak reddish-brown rock, and a arduous scramble onto a crowded peak. But when the sky is clear the exertion is worthwhile. From the summit it is just about possible to make out the Pacific, more than fifty kilometers to the east, its rippled surface polished by the morning sun's rays. And if one turns full circle on the highest point on Taiwan, mountain ranges appear to radiate outwards like the spokes of a wheel. North and south they march as far as the horizon.

On holiday mornings the motley-hued jackets and hats of the assembled hikers give the peak a quilted appearance. Some squat in nooks to escape the biting gale; others collect photographic evidence of their achievement, typically by posing beside the bust of Yu You-renn. Various structures have been built on the summit of Jade Mountain: Each one has reflected the political reality of its era. The Japanese *jinja* Shinto shrine was demolished by Chinese Nationalists in 1945. Two decades later the memorial to Yu – statesman, journalist, calligrapher and ally of Chiang Kai-shek – was erected. Gazing in the direction of the province from which Yu originated, the monument represents a desire to return to and reunite with the mainland. This symbolism enrages pro-independence activists: The statue was vandalized in the mid-1990s.*

Few hikers go further than the summit. After admiring the scenery for as long as they could endure the cold, most retreat back down the path they had climbed in pre-dawn darkness. Some energetic individuals set off in the direction of Jade Mountain's north peak and the manned weather station thereon. This time around I noted that we four seemed to be the only people making the northeasterly descent towards Patungkuan. With Richard I had gone this way two-and-a-half years previously. After that trek I had vowed, "never again." The trail had been terrifyingly precipitous then, and having witnessed the destruction wrought elsewhere in the mountains by subsequent typhoons, I doubted it would be passable this time. But the ropes and harnesses we carried placated my fears. I walked nurturing a small flame of confidence.

* This expedition took place in November 1996. In the summer of 1998 the bust of Yu You-renn was replaced with a much smaller monolith bearing only the Chinese characters *yu-shan*, "jade mountain," and the summit's height in meters. It seems Yu's memorial was smashed and the debris unceremoniously thrown down the mountainside. Before the cement on the new monument had dried, an aboriginal woman used her finger to add to it the word "Batongkon" – the name of the mountain in her tribal tongue.

For an hour the four of us worked our way downward through cool, pristine alpine forest. The trail was rough and strewn with small, gun-metal gray rocks as awkward to walk over as golf balls. For the first time on our expedition we could neither see nor hear other humans.

Soon we arrived at a rudimentary campground beside a small stream. Half-burned, half- decomposed trash overflowed from a barrel. But when I turned my back on this detritus, the spot became sublime.

At valley's end the main peak of Jade Mountain towered massively. Around us were trees which had survived for centuries if not millennia. While the others sunbathed, I explored a dank patch of forest. I found rocks dressed in lichen and thick patches of moss.

Knowing that the most hair-raising stretch of path still lay ahead made it difficult to relax. But when we came to the landslides which had swept half-a-dozen sections of the trail into the gorge far below, I found myself undaunted. Remarkably, no major deterioration seemed to have taken place, and I was more experienced, more sure-footed than before. We slithered across the powdery, unstable gradients without incident, and reached Patungkuan with a good amount of daylight left.

An alpine meadow encircled by forested peaks, Patung-kuan is perhaps the only place in Taiwan where there is less human traffic now than a century ago. The vale has only ever been accessible by foot, though for some decades after 1875 a migration route passed through here. The Patungkuan Old Trail was used by Han families moving from the west of the island to the thinly populated east coast. Stretches of the Old Trail are still extant, but these days they are trodden only by National Park rangers and a few adventurous hikers.

Having settled that we would go no further until the next

morning, we erected our tents at Patungkuan and held a brief confab about routes. We decided on our next objective.

I agreed when Eric said, "What I like about Taiwan is that it's finite." But Taiwan's modest dimensions are deceptive: The island has no deserts or howling wastes, but there are mountains and valleys so inaccessible and so seldom visited they might just as well be a thousand kilometers from the nearest city.

We enjoyed a brief purple twilight as the sun sank behind Jade Mountain. I was tired out after the early start we had made that day, but slept fitfully. And each time I awoke, I seemed to hear a light rain falling, or the canine yaps of barking deer scrounging for food.

We rose well after dawn and wasted half the morning. The four of us finally assembled on the path and began to march deeper into the National Park. In shaded corners the grasses and ferns dripped with dew. The morning mist gave way to sunshine. We negotiated fallen trees and trickling streams, and delighted in a pine-needle covered footpath which was broad and flat. Shod in decent boots and carrying lightweight camping equipment, I tried to imagine what the pioneers who blazed this trail had gone through. They would have traveled barefoot, encumbered by the possessions needed to start a new life. Many would have posted watch after dark for fear of beasts and head-hunters. They would never have understood my motives for entering this wilderness.

Unable to cross a river where we had hoped to, we revised our route to include two abandoned gold mines marked on our maps. These places had long intrigued me; but I have never been able to find out just when they were worked, or whether any men made their fortunes out here.

We reached the first by mid-afternoon. A wooden hut stood there, but it was obviously a new structure built for hikers and park rangers. There was no evidence of people having dug or panned for gold. I tried to visualize Chinese men in conical hats squatting at the stream's edge, sieving hopefully. I scanned the nearby hillsides for evidence of human workings, but concluded that foliage would have covered any scars long ago.

The following day was sunny. The stretch of trail was the most challenging yet; some of the steps up were almost insurmountable. In several places I gripped gnarled roots and pulled myself upwards, acutely aware that the weight of my backpack could easily send me tumbling to disaster. But we were richly rewarded for our exertions. Paiyang Gold Mine is more than 3,500 meters above sea level: From it we had an eagle's eye view over a vast and unspoiled valley. Beneath us was a sea of evergreens. Above us loomed the rocky peak of Hsiukuluanshan, Taiwan's third-highest mountain.

We set up camp in the lee of an ancient-looking, open-sided shelter made of slate and well-seasoned timber. A few yards away a crystalline waterfall spilled into a natural bathtub. We found what might have been the entrance to a mine. After a couple of hours of dallying at this splendid spot I had regained the energy and inclination to climb further up, towards the summit of Hsiukuluanshan. But by then our eyrie was lost in fog.

Opening the tent unveiled a morning as misty as the evening before. For a whole day we strayed nary a hundred meters from the shelter. We read to one another, wandered, washed in freezing water, and welcomed the chores of cooking and cleaning our metal pans.

The second morning was no better: thick mist, a light drizzle. At least there were no high winds. We broke camp with a speed and decisiveness which would have served us well had we managed it earlier in the expedition. After two hours' walking on empty stomachs, we cooked up an extravagant breakfast. Certain that we would return to civilization within a day, we had no reason to husband our provisions. Besides, the more we ate, the less we would have to carry. Eric blazed on ahead: We caught up with him at Patungkuan. Before our arrival he had spotted a barking deer foraging, unusually, in broad daylight. When I asked him if he had managed to capture it on film, he shook his head sadly.

A little sunshine broke through the cloud cover as we headed toward the aboriginal village and hot springs resort of Tungpu. We realized that covering the remaining kilometers before sunset was impossible, but we were determined not to spend another night in damp sleeping bags. We pushed on at a pace just short of running.

For much of the time it felt as though we were moving through a tunnel of thick vegetation. Whenever I came across breaks in the canopy I paused and gazed down the valley in wonderment. Dusk was stupendously beautiful. The far side of the valley darkened until it was a vast canvas of black. Distant mountains became blurred aquamarine triangles.

Footsore and exhausted, we covered the final few hundred meters to Tungpu at a convalescent pace. Had there been onlookers, we would have seemed a sorry sight. But there were none: At eight in the evening the resort's main street was deserted. Almost every business had shuttered down for the night, but we found a not-quite-closed restaurant, and prevailed upon the owner to cook steaming portions of fried rice for us. Then at the youth hostel we discovered an upside to the typhoon weather which had pushed us out of the mountains. It had scared off other visitors: we had the dormitory and its swimming pool to ourselves. We felt deserving of the luxury.

The next morning we tried to hitch back to Alishan. There was a depressing paucity of traffic, but finally a black four-wheel-drive Suzuki stopped. The driver wound down his window: It was the aboriginal policeman Eric and I had met seven days earlier.

He took us to Tzuchung and invited us into the back of the police station. One of his colleagues, a Han Chinese, was relaxing there. A gas fire added to the air of conviviality. Over cups of green tea we exchanged stories of mountains climbed, disasters averted and wild animals seen. "We have to carry guns when we go on foot patrol," the Bunun officer told us. "Hungry black bears are the main danger…"

DEER HARBOR

I was targeted the moment I entered the passenger car. As soon as I located my seat a young woman began to drift closer, smiling as if I was an old acquaintance. I tried to figure out where I might have met her. Before addressing me she spoke softly to the middle-aged, bespectacled man beside me. I caught some of what she said: She was asking the man if they could exchange seats so she could talk to the foreigner. He muttered assent, picked up his magazine, and without ever having said a word to me, squeezed past to the aisle.

The woman then spoke to me: "Can I sit here and talk to you, sir?" Her confident smile gave way to an imploring look. Not feeling particularly sociable, I shrugged as if to say, "up to you." The moment she sat down, the train resumed its northward journey.

"Where are you going, sir?" Question followed predictable question. She was indefatigable. Some foreign residents describe this kind of person as a "language rapist" – a Taiwanese who engages each and every Westerner he or she set eyes on in the hope of an impromptu English lesson. A realization that I would not get any reading done before Changhua soon settled over me.

*   *   *

Just before Changhua there is a small town called Ershui. I should like to live there. Each time I pass through it on the train, it strikes me as idyllic: a checker-board of old houses, rice paddies and betel-nut plantations, cleft by waterways, bound together by narrow ribbons of tarmac. Watermelons swell and ripen on frames; water buffalo loaf in a timeless rural torpor.

There are hills within sight of Ershui. And on the day I went to Changhua to meet Hui-ju, streaks of mist draped over them had created a vista as beautiful as any I have seen in classical Chinese paintings.

* * *

Hui-ju's remarkable English-language ability was apparent the first time I met her. She led the questioning when her high school's English club reconvened with me as its new teacher. Her audacity left me floundering. "Don't you think Christianity is stupid?" she asked.

I gave an agnostic, non-committal reply, and then asked her to answer her own question. In pitch-perfect American tones, she did so without hesitating: "I think Christianity is stupid. Christians believe that Mary gave birth to Jesus even though she never had sex with a man. That's impossible!" She squeezed a scathing amount of condescension into the two last words.

A few years after that unforgettable encounter, I read Love and Faith, a collection of speeches and articles by former President Lee Teng-hui. I found that the very same conundrum had for years prevented Lee from accepting Christianity. When he ceased, as he put it, "looking at spiritual questions from a biological perspective," he became the fervent believer he is today.

* * *

Changhua station was teeming with Filipino and Thai guest workers. Amidst them, looking nervous, was Hui-ju. After exchanging pleasantries we walked across the road to the bus station. Within minutes we were on our way to the coast.

Lukang – its name translates as "Deer Harbor" – was once a significant port. In addition to deer hides and meat, rice was exported to the mainland. At the end of the eighteenth century Lukang was Taiwan's second largest town. As recently as 1896, only Taipei, Tainan and Chiayi were more populous. Now it has around 30,000 inhabitants. It went into decline when silting prevented larger vessels from using the port, and rice surpluses shrank as Taiwan's population grew. The Japanese closed the harbor to cross-strait trade. Prosperity has never returned on any scale, so there has been little redevelopment. Consequently much of the town's traditional architecture has survived intact.

Hui-ju and I began by roaming the length of Chungshan Road, the main thoroughfare. Dozens of two-story shophouses in the center of town still bear, on their uppermost floors, the surname crests of the original occupants. Family names were especially important in the Lukang of yesteryear. The three most numerous – Shih, Huang and Hsu – constituted rival clans. These groups were often at daggers drawn, but they found a novel way of managing their enmity. Once a year, the young men of each clan would gather for a daylong rock fight. Between these clashes feuding was prohibited. There were no official winners in the three-way battles. Teeth got broken; sometimes a man's eye would be put out. When the Japanese authorities tried to abolish this tradition, the locals responded in a characteristically Taiwanese manner: They ignored the ban and moved their yearly fracas out into the countryside, far from any officious bureaucrats. No rock fights, it seems, have occurred since World War II.

Some of the workshops on Chungshan Road have been producing the same goods for more than a century: ornate wooden palanquins which are beautiful but much too delicate for the rough-and-tumble of many religious parades; ceremonial vessels made of tin and silver; ancestor shrines; hand-painted paper lanterns; icons and images of popular deities. An irresistible juxtaposing of old and new prompted me to take a photograph: Beside a pair of freshly carved and as yet unpainted palanquins, there stood a rusting motorcycle.

Lukang has an abundance of temples. Before reaching its most famous house of worship we came across a small shrine squeezed between two merchant's houses. No one was there, but the offerings of fruit and incense were fresh. When I commented that soot had blackened some of the calligraphy panels to the point of illegibility, Hui-ju chided me: "You shouldn't say, 'it's dirty.' You should say: 'a lot of incense has been burned here.' People consider that a good thing."

Lungshan Temple resembles many temples in Communist China. I felt this the moment I stepped into the forecourt. It looks its age (two hundred and some years), and feels like a museum. Nowadays it is more of a tourist attraction than a place of worship. It would, I think, appeal to those Westerners who romantically imagine Chinese temples to be places of placid contemplation.

Most visitors come to Lungshan to admire the ceiling. One section is indeed a masterpiece: Subtly colorful wooden beams converge on an exquisite painting of a dragon's head. Elsewhere, despite strip lighting, the interior is full of shadows. While I was there an old woman came in and mumbled a series of prayers. In the gloom, the glowing tips of her joss sticks looked like a swarm of fireflies. Her invocations were undoubtedly sincere, but did little to dispel the somber emptiness of the place.

The Queen of Heaven Temple, Lukang's principal Matsu shrine, was entirely different: a cauldron of people, noise and smoke. A king's ransom in spirit money lay stacked from floor to ceiling. Red offertory tables covered with food blocked the aisles. Surveying the chaos from above was a kitschy animatronic tiger. The Year of The Tiger had only just begun, but all this animal could do was shake his head wearily.

We squeezed through the throng and climbed the stairs to the temple's first floor, hoping that it would be less crowded. We were disappointed. There seemed to be just as many people, and much of the floor space was occupied by huge conical fixtures which revolved slowly. Each cone glittered with hundreds of tiny lights, and would not have looked out of place in a discotheque. The bulbs represented donations made to the temple, and symbolized the good luck now flowing to each donor as a result of his or her generosity.

A battalion of volunteer workers swept the floors and plucked incense sticks from the censers standing before each god. Their eagerness to clean up was such that Matsu and her cohorts could have got only the briefest whiff of each sacrifice before it was snatched away. In a side office, clerks pored over sprawling ledgers, tallying donations and totting up sales. A young man restocked a vending machine which dispensed not votive items but soft drinks. A middle-aged woman prayed earnestly; a few meters away a man growled into his cell phone. By now I was used to such things, and saw all this not as a clash or contradiction, but as part of a natural, ongoing confluence of the sacred and the profane.

PEIKANG'S CHAOTIENGONG

Chinese migrants began to cross the Taiwan Strait in large numbers in the seventeenth century. They called their destination "Treasure Island." This was no mere expression of hope: The name was apt. Compared to the hard-scrabble regions most of them came from, Taiwan was indeed bountiful. The soil was fertile and well watered; the land was heavily forested; wildlife was abundant.

Not every settler came in search of a better life, however. Some were fugitives. In 1563, a pirate leader called Lin Tao-chien dropped anchor in the broad estuary of the Peikang River, north of modern-day Chiayi. Ming Dynasty naval forces had forced Lin to flee Fujian. A few years later he sailed away and resumed his ravaging of the mainland's coastline, but some of his followers are thought to have stayed. Their descendants and later migrants who joined them transformed the plains either side of the river into a terraqueous landscape of rice paddies and fish farms.

Before traveling to the small town that takes its name from the Peikang River, I learned the area had been playing a gruesome role in Taiwan's vast and varied black economy. It had become a center for the illegal dolphin meat trade. Dolphin flesh is in great demand: It is considered both a delicacy and a health food. If eaten raw, is it believed to boost men's masculine qualities, and enhance women's femininity. A police crackdown in Peikang had netted six tonnes of dolphin meat. A local man was caught red-handed butchering one of the mammals; a third of a tonne of dolphin meat was found in his van. It was his second conviction for offenses against protected creatures, so the penalty was severe: seven years' jail and a fine of NT$2.5 million. It is fitting, perhaps, that Peikang's putative founder was a notorious pirate.

Hui-ju accompanied me to Peikang. We did not go directly to the town's most famous structure, the Chaotiengong. Our first stop was a little shrine called Yi Min Temple. It was built two hundred years ago to commemorate 36 of Peikang's citizens – and one dog – who died defending the community.

The two centuries which followed the Manchu recovery of Taiwan were violent times. Elsewhere in the Chinese Empire the island was disparaged as a place where, "a minor revolt happens every three years, and a major revolt every five." Many of these uprisings were led by sworn brotherhoods or secret societies. Clan rivalries and land disputes were the cause of many clashes. Banditry was rife; aboriginal raids were frequent. Many communities organized militias. Peikang's was highly effective until one night in May 1786. Previously a faithful guard dog had raised the alarm whenever strangers approached the township, giving the garrison time to ready themselves. But on that fateful night the canine was fed poison, and a band of brigands entered Peikang undetected. Three dozen men were massacred as they slept: Their remains lie in two mass graves behind the shrine. The dog has its own tomb nearby, and there is an altar dedicated to it inside Yi Min Temple. Some say the Chinese are unsentimental about their animals, but this dog's loyalty has not been forgotten.

It was a short walk through quiet streets to the Chaotiengong. This temple is not especially large, but it is one of the oldest Matsu shrines in Taiwan. It has been added to, renovated and reconstructed several times since 1694.

Inside, Hui-ju and I saw the usual accouterments: idols; a votive bell shaped like an axe; and petitions written out on slips of pink paper and left on the various altars. Amidst the gods and demigods we found carved depictions of eighteenth-century

European traders – balding, pasty-faced men in breeches, pot bellies spilling over their belts. The most interesting artifact is in a small courtyard behind the main altar. Embedded in one well-worn stone step there is a tiny iron nail: We would have missed this relic but for the dab of red paint highlighting it. A plaque relates that two centuries ago, one of Matsu's devotees knelt at this very spot and prayed because he had been told that his parents had been lost at sea. He asked the Sea Goddess if he would ever see them again. His manner of prognostication was unusual: He held a nail in one hand and struck it with a mallet. When the soft iron penetrated the much harder stone, he knew Matsu was telling him he should not give up hope. According to legend, he was later reunited with his parents.

Having entered through a side doorway, I failed to notice the leaflets and booklets stacked up behind the main entrance until we were about to leave. An elderly janitor watched over these piles of literature. He looked up at me, then at Hui-ju, and asked her: "Can your friend read Chinese?"

"A little." Her reply seemed to satisfy the caretaker. Slowly he selected three or four publications for me.

I thanked the caretaker and spent a moment perusing what he had given me. That so many dignitaries have visited the Chaotiengong and made sacrifices here is obviously a source of pride for the temple's management committee. Color photographs in one booklet showed former Premier Hau Pei-tsun offering incense to the Sea Goddess, former Vice President Lien Chan presenting an inscribed panel to the temple, and former President Lee Teng-hui standing before the main altar, paying his respects to Matsu. Lee, of course, is an enthusiastic Christian. But obviously he thought it wise to publicly honor the goddess so many of his compatriots revere.

TAINAN

Dutch traders occupied Tainan between 1624 and 1662. Their legacy includes two small forts and, some locals maintain, a predisposition towards reddish hair in the gene pool. I visited both forts: Little remains of one; the other failed to excite me.

The story of the Dutch colony is more interesting than the physical evidence it left behind. Formosa was thinly populated in the early 1600s. In addition to aborigines, there were a few thousand Chinese farmers and their families on the island. The Dutch needed labor, so the VOC (the Dutch United East India Company) encouraged immigration. Seeds, tools and oxen were offered as incentives. Droves of landless Fujianese peasants crossed the strait and settled on Taiwan. The population multiplied; business boomed. Ships brought whale oil, satin, velvet and linen from the Netherlands, and carried silks and porcelain back to Europe. Local commodities such as camphor, sugar, rice and deerskins were exported to the mainland and Japan. Woods and peppers from Southeast Asia passed through the colony. Amber, lead, tin and opium were traded.

The number of European residents never exceeded 3,000. With the soldiers, sailors and merchants were a handful of Protestant pastors. These intrepid missionaries were successful in converting many members of the lowland tribes, but when their zeal (which included whipping and banishing idolaters, adulterers and fornicators) began to upset non-Christian aborigines and the vehemently anti-Christian Japanese traders, they were quickly reined in by the colony's authorities. Like the

Dutch outpost on Dejima near Nagasaki (where crosses were trampled each year to satisfy Japanese sensibilities), the Taiwan settlement was first and foremost a commercial venture.

The Dutch did little to endear themselves to the locals. They taxed heavily and conscripted arbitrarily. Whenever they faced an uprising, the "red-haired barbarians" did not hesitate to kill large numbers of people. Their nemesis was a half-Japanese warrior considered a great Chinese patriot. European chronicles of the time refer to him by his Fujianese name, Koxinga; but most Chinese know him as Cheng Cheng-kung. He led 400 ships and 30,000 soldiers (including two companies of black Africans) to Taiwan in 1661, and lay siege to the Dutch forts. The foreigners resisted until their provisions were exhausted. They handed over 471,000 guilders, and were allowed to withdraw to Java.

(Koxinga's reputation as Taiwan's liberator is founded on his successful eviction of the Dutch from their bases in south and north Taiwan. It seems churlish to point out that some historians attribute the defeat of the Dutch to the failure of two relief expeditions sent from Jakarta – the first was led by an overcautious commander, while the second ran into bad weather. Moreover, Koxinga's forces were unable to secure the island against European penetration: In 1663 the Dutch easily retook Keelung, and maintained a garrison there for five years. This outpost was abandoned for commercial, not military, reasons.)

A Ming Dynasty loyalist, Koxinga was more concerned with his enemies on the mainland than with the Europeans. For the better part of two decades he had been fighting the Manchu, whom he regarded as foreign usurpers from the north. In 1644, a Manchu (Qing) emperor was enthroned. Remnants of the old regime fought on, but they were unable to stem the Manchu advance. The Ming cause was weakened by defections: Koxinga's own father went over to the Qing in 1646. After a military debacle in southern China, Koxinga and his dwindling band of die-hards withdrew to the coast of Fujian, and thence to

Taiwan.

As Chiang Kai-shek would a few hundred years later, Koxinga promised that he would soon return to the mainland and restore the "legitimate" regime. But he went insane and died within a year of expelling the Dutch. (Two centuries after his death, and with the approval of Qing officials, he was declared a god.) There are other parallels between Koxinga and the generalissimo. Both men ran authoritarian governments – under Koxinga's rule cutting bamboo without permission was punishable by death – but at the same time encouraged economic development and, with the assistance of refugee intellectuals, bolstered the island's Chinese cultural identity. Both Koxinga and Chiang were succeeded by their sons. And both would have been dismayed by later developments. Koxinga's grandson surrendered Taiwan to the Qing in 1683; by the mid-1990s, the Kuomintang was led by Lee Teng-hui – a man whose enthusiasm for reunification was so obviously lukewarm that some accused him of secreting plotting Taiwan's independence.

Determined to preserve Ming traditions, scholars in Koxinga's entourage founded several cultural institutions. Their greatest legacy is Tainan's Confucius Temple. Entering the grounds of this crimson-pink building is like falling through a trapdoor into a different world. There is a serenity about it which is priceless. The clutter and tumult found in most temples is absent; the interior verges on the austere. No idols reside under the eaves of this or any other Confucian shrine. Neither incense nor ghost money are burned here, and ceremonies are held just once a year – at dawn on September 28, the birthday of the Great Sage.

In spite of his preeminent position in Chinese culture and the temples dedicated to him, Confucius has never been formally promoted to godhood. The Sage is regarded as the single most famous cultural figure in China's history, yet in Taiwan it is hard to see his influence. Local people seldom mention Confucius, or cite his doctrines. Among the skills he asked his students to master were archery and charioteering. In modern Taiwan, however, soldiering is disdained, and the standard of driving is abysmal.

*　　　　*　　　　*

In the heart of Tainan there are mazes of lanes, and alleys barely wide enough for two bicycles to pass. I loved exploring these back streets, and not only to admire the old brick or stucco houses. This is where traditional life survives, where three or more generations live under the same roof, and where the front room of every second house is given over to a family shrine bedecked with icons and offerings. Some shrines are festooned with Christmas tree lights, but more usually the only illumination is an electric candle that is never turned off. Walking through such neighborhoods late at night, I found the glow from these red lamps both eerie and comforting.

These alleyways are productive. Housewives and grand-parents sit in doorways doing piecework for local manufacturers. ("Our living rooms are our factories," a government official once said). From many buildings spill the sounds of industry – pressing, molding, stamping. Within fifty meters of one apartment I lived in there was an iron foundry, a playing-cards factory and a furniture workshop.

Traditional businesses survive: noodle and tofu makers (the latter are usually at their busiest in the hours before dawn; the former drape their output over the rickety wooden frames); calligraphers who write good-luck couplets for weddings; barbers, cobblers and seal makers. Once I came across a sidewalk beautician whose customers were arrayed on chairs up and down the lane. Swathed in towels, coated in rejuvenating creams, they had, like a harvest, been put out to dry in the sun.

*   *   *

Certain noises epitomize Tainan's residential areas: the hum of air-conditioning; the drone of ventilators sucking greasy smoke out of kitchens; and the crunching sound of iron shutters being drawn down as stores close and families seal themselves in for the night. This last action, ritually equivalent to raising a drawbridge, symbolizes the cultural gulf between the city's traditionally minded mainstream – families whose evenings are occupied by work, study or TV – and more streetwise individuals who enjoy the city's nightlife.

*   *   *

Tainan has its desirable and undesirable neighborhoods, but compared to North American or European cities, the economic and social disparities between one part of the municipality and another are insignificant.

One sometimes finds conspicuously opulent homes beside dilapidated shacks. In the same alleyway it is possible to find one family with considerable inherited wealth, another that is nouveau riche, and an elderly couple who survive by extracting recyclable materials from other people's garbage. There has been no great middle-class flight to the suburbs – partly because the suburbs are less attractive and less convenient places to live, but also because the most popular schools are found close to the city center.

In recent years several of Tainan's roads have been widened. In many places this has been encouraged by local residents who hope that making their properties more accessible will boost real estate values. But on an island where people are already short of living space, it seems wrong to surrender more and more land to motor vehicles.

One of the oldest streets anywhere in Taiwan, Yenping

Street, was widened a few years ago for commercial reasons. This resulted in the partial or complete demolition of a number of very old houses, an act denounced by conservationists as vandalism. These days Yenping Street is noticeably more prosperous – eateries, hairdressing salons and other businesses have appeared – but the thoroughfare's appearance is spoiled by the many wrecked buildings. These were brutally truncated in the road- widening process; several have yet to be repaired, and have a bombed-out, abandoned look to them. This cannot be what the planners had in mind.

Fortunately, some of Tainan's streets – including two which run parallel to Yenping Street – retain a great deal of their traditional personality. But many of the old houses are unoccupied. Others are inhabited by elderly people unable or unwilling to keep up their properties. Behind facades bearing protective "sword-lion" emblems, one often finds dwellings in a state of utter collapse. No effort, it seems, is made to gentrify these old houses; this is something that astonishes Western visitors. It seems likely that, within a generation, these quaint neighborhoods will have completely disappeared.

*　　　*　　　*

It took me years to get inside the East Mountain Temple. When I first arrived in Tainan sightseeing was not a priority. Later the building was closed for renovation. When, finally, I got to see the interior and the shrine's famous Hell murals, I felt a little disappointed.

The panels depict terrified wretches being dragged before the underworld's fearsome magistrates, and many of the excruciating punishments meted out to wrongdoers: naked sinners lashed to red-hot smokestacks; dropped onto spikes; cut in half; fed to wild animals; ground between millstones; forced to imbibe scalding liquids; or hammered, stabbed, enucleated and eviscerated. But compared to the visions of Hieronymous Bosch and other European artists, these monochrome scenes on are neither especially powerful nor memorable. Far more intriguing are the notices posted by the Ministry of the Interior, forbidding certain rituals. No one could tell me precisely what rites are prohibited, but having seen what is allowed in other temples, I guessed it had to be something terrifying, or downright dangerous.

Beside the East Mountain Temple there is, aptly, a workshop which turns out funerary items: mock houses burned to ensure that the dead person does not lack for shelter in the next world; paper furniture to equip the deceased's abode; cars, bicycles and suitcases. These goods are made to order. Often the kin of the departed have to anticipate what their loved ones will need. But some people, before they die, describe to their relatives exactly what they will need in Heaven. In either case, posthumous infusions of cash – bundles of spirit money consigned to the flames – are also necessary.

Joss sticks or special supplies are required for most religious rites. Outside famous temples, there are usually hawkers peddling the necessary articles. Nowadays many supermarkets stock spirit money (gold for deities, silver for ancestors), but for other traditional items – those used in weddings, funerals and the construction of family shrines – people turn to specialist shops. In Tainan, such stores are concentrated near the East Mountain Temple on Minchuan Road.

In some of these, fifty or more kinds of joss sticks are arranged, like candy, in plastic bins. The sticks vary greatly in length and thickness, but almost all are bright red – a color which connotes good luck and happiness. All the accouterments needed to construct a household shrine are sold hereabouts: ornately carved tables; vessels in which incense is burned; colorful, embroidered tablecloths used when food sacrifices are set out; and the red electric candles which burn, all night long, in millions of Taiwanese homes. There are huge candles half as big as a man, and spirit-money burners ranging in size from small, portable models to impressive furnaces which can only be moved by crane.

Swords, axes and spiked wooden clubs used by *tang-ki* – spirit mediums who, while possessed by gods, slash and cut themselves – are displayed alongside everyday products like red wrapping paper and candles. The function of other goods is less obvious. Amidst old-fashioned conical hats and bamboo-handled brooms are what foreigners might assume to be ordinary baskets. These hampers sport red hoops and are never, in fact, used for shopping. Worshipers carry ritual items and sacrificial gifts to temple in them, or employ them in betrothal ceremonies.

Some business advertise "gods' clothes." The gods in question are the idols that reside in temples. Many such josses are tiny – no bigger than dolls. But regardless of size or eminence, Chinese gods must be properly attired. This means sumptuous, brightly-colored jackets and fantastically ornate headgear.

Religious idols can be purchased from the workshops where they are carved. When not dealing with customers, the craftsmen are busy sanding and lacquering figurines of Buddha or statuettes of Kuanyin. Images of gods are manufactured, traded – and sometimes stolen. The transparent plastic screens installed in many temples are there, I was told, to stop thefts. (In 1995, a 160-year-old icon was taken from Taipei's Wufu Temple. In its place, the janitor found a ransom note demanding NT$500,000. The joss was never returned.)

*   *   *

For a while I lived in a tenth-floor flat overlooking one of the city's oldest neighborhoods. Several times each weekend, amplified, distorted skirling would herald the approach of a religious parade or a funeral cortege. Whenever a procession passed beneath my window, the droning pipes, thunderous gongs and firecracker barrages made conversation impossible. Every time I watched the vehicles inch their way forward, I was struck by the sovereign disregard such convoys showed for red lights and road etiquette. Traffic laws do not to apply, it seems, to the deified or the dead.

*   *   *

There is little evidence of it today, but Tainan was once a walled city. The defenses were built in the first quarter of the eighteenth century after a series of uprisings had threatened Manchu control of the island.

Two of the old city gates survive in their original locations. Road widening has left the Great East Gate stranded in the middle of a busy traffic circle. The Great South Gate exists in more prepossessing surroundings, however: It has been restored and made the centerpiece of a small park.

The gate itself is handsome, but far more interesting are the inscribed stone slabs which have been gathered from around the city and put on display in the park. Some of these stele were erected to commemorate wealthy citizens who funded public works. Others were put up by the authorities to promulgate new laws. One of the latter, dating from 1767, decrees that beggars shall not display corpses when soliciting alms. This method of generating sympathy must have been popular, as almost a century later another attempt to outlaw the practice was made. In 1840, the government announced that female domestic servants should be married by the age of 25; they placed the onus of finding a suitable spouse on the maid's employer. Edicts from the same era required soldiers not to extort money from civilians, militiamen not to rob merchant ships, and government officials not to enrich themselves at the expense of the citizenry. Such rules were ineffectual, in part because civil servants from continental China regarded Taiwan as a hardship posting and one which indicated they were unlikely to rise any further in the imperial bureaucracy. Many mandarins consoled themselves by making illegal fortunes. The endemic corruption was noticed by foreign residents, among them Mackay (officials, he writes, had "itching palms") and Pickering, who devoted an entire chapter of Pioneering in Formosa to the problem.

*   *   *

Hsiaopei, the city's largest night market, is a good place to slurp snake soup, and on weekends the crowds of shoppers are joined by quacks and monks. The mountebanks are hyperactive and highly entertaining as they push supplements, tonics, hair restoratives and aphrodisiacs. The monks use different tactics to make themselves conspicuous: silence and stasis. Despite the crowds heaving around them they maintain rigid postures. And while holding out their alms-bowls, they somehow manage to look more bored than suppliant.

Apart from monks, Taiwan has few beggars. While at train or bus stations, I would sometimes find myself face-to-face with a derelict. These people are almost always male, often old, and usually mentally troubled rather than physically disabled. Considering that the government makes few provisions for its unemployed, aged and disabled citizens, the number of truly destitute people is impressively low. Charities exist, but families form the main safety net.

Many Westerners, and some Taiwanese, believe that the Chinese are inherently more industrious and entrepreneurial than other races. But one of my students gave me a more prosaic explanation of why his compatriots work so hard: "We always worry that something bad will happen – bad health, an accident, a war. So everyone thinks they should save a lot of money. People in Western countries can rely on their governments to help them.

We have to rely on ourselves and our families."

(There can be no doubt that Taiwanese people work more hours per year than their Western counterparts, but it is also true that some of them begin working unusually late in life. I taught English to a number of young men from well-off families who, having attended college, done their military service, and then rested for a while, were 27 or 28 when they did paid work for the first time in their lives.)

Taiwanese people have gleaned that young Westerners think nothing of defying their parents' advice, and that many unmarried couples openly cohabit. But what really shocked my students were the anecdotes I told of acquaintances in Britain who had been kicked out of the family home by their own parents. Such evictions are almost unknown in Taiwan, where families seem to be more tolerant and indulgent than those in the West. Almost everyone with close relatives can count on aid when they need it.

Observers rightfully praise this aspect of life in Taiwan, but sometimes the results are less than fair. A factory owner told me about his sister: "She and her husband dealt in land. They made a lot of money, but then the market turned and they went bust. She came to me for a small loan. Being my sister, I was happy to lend her some money, and I didn't care if she paid me back or not. I lent her money three or four times. She never repaid any of it. When she telephoned again asking for money, I told her that she could come and work in my factory – I'm always looking for workers. I even offered to pay her more than the women who've been working here for a long time. She got angry. She said, 'I'm a businesswoman, not a factory worker!'"

I asked him if he then stopped supporting his sister: "No. I have to give her money whenever she says she needs some. My mother expects it."

Taiwanese attitudes seem to have created a reasonably effective safety net which is not a disincentive to work. Still, I am sure that if a comprehensive welfare system were established, the vast majority of Taiwanese people would work just as hard as they do now. During his stint as a UK government minister in the 1980s, Lord Gowrie searched the register of unemployed in the United Kingdom for Chinese names. He was unable to find one.

*   *   *

The air quality around my wife's home village in Tainan County is good, and would be even better were it not for farmers' bonfires, housewives cooking on wood-fired stoves, and everyone burning ghost money on festival days.

One time, after watching my wife and her brother pray beside their grandmother's grave, and then set fire to a stack of spirit money, I asked why they didn't just burn a spirit credit card instead. It would be cheaper, and much better for the environment.

The logic of my wife's reply was unassailable: "My grandmother couldn't read or write. She wouldn't know how to sign her name."

*   *   *

Fengshui, a Mandarin term meaning "wind and water," has entered the English language, and the ancient practice it describes has caught on in the West. A way of gauging the harmony between five traditional elements – metal, fire, wood, water and earth – the custom attributes success or failure to mysterious cosmic forces. Strategically placed objects can supposedly attract beneficial flows of energy; ill-considered design may have the opposite effect.

Anecdotal evidence suggests that many Taiwanese fear bad fengshui. One student told me that her grandfather moved house on the advice of a geomancer, who had told him that his chronic health problems resulted from certain characteristics of the bungalow he had grown up in. An English teacher – a devout Christian – showed me a house he had bought and would use for his cram school, and gloated how he had gotten it cheap because the building's bad fengshui had repelled other potential buyers. (Within a year his business slumped badly, and he sold the house.) After a China Airlines jet crashed while attempting to land at Taipei's international airport in 1998, killing more than 200 people including the governor of Taiwan's Central Bank, articles in the local press implied that the calamity happened because of the disastrous positioning of the Central Bank's headquarters. And as soon as Chen Shui-bian was declared winner of the 2000 presidential election, fengshui experts began seeking explanations for his victory. Various geographical features in and around his home village near Kuantien in Tainan County were identified as being critical to his success, and the house he grew up in became a bona fide tourist attraction.

*   *   *

The road between Shanshang and Shanhua, two small towns in Tainan County, would offer a timeless picture of rural Taiwan – were it not for a pair of massive factories dominating the skyline, and Thai-language signs advertising a karaoke parlor. Thai, Filipino and Indonesian enclaves have become fixtures in several districts which, until a few years ago, were homogeneous communities. The arrival of foreign laborers has been the biggest and most sudden change to Taiwan's ethnic makeup since the Nationalists retreated from the mainland in 1949, bringing with them two million soldiers and civilians.

Foreign maids and caregivers are distributed fairly evenly around the island. But factory hands – usually hired in large numbers by major enterprises – tend to be concentrated in industrial zones outside the cities. The influx of Southeast Asians has, consequently, had a greater impact on places like Shanshang than on Taipei, which has long played host to a sizable foreign population.

Driving through the outskirts of Kuantien, my wife and I spotted a group of young Thai men gathered outside a bustling shop, cheering and booing as they watched kick-boxing matches on a large TV set.

The proprietor of the store and its associated businesses – a karaoke joint and a small restaurant – turned out to be an ethnic Chinese from Thailand. (Overseas Chinese are given visa privileges denied other foreigners. Some foreigners see this as blatant racism: I regard it as equivalent to Israel's Law of Return.) The signboards out front were in Thai script only; the restaurant's menu was equally monolingual. I thought it ironic that sophisticated city dwellers pay a premium to enjoy Thai food in downtown restaurants, when much cheaper – and probably more authentic – fare is available in rural backwaters like this. In addition to instant noodles and crackers imported from Thailand, the shop stocked some of the ingredients which give Thai cuisine its distinctive tang – dried coconut cream, lemon grass, dried kaffir lime leaves and dried rhizone – plus CDs and tapes of Thai pop music, videos, newspapers and magazines, balms, lotions, airmail paper and envelopes.

Chehang, site of another large industrial estate, had four Thai-oriented businesses on a single street. The smallest was a simple convenience store whose owner had found that setting a couple of folding tables and some plastic stools in front of his store was good for business. There being few entertainment options in the area, his shop had become a place where off-duty workers would congregate. A supermarket down the road issued me with a trilingual plastic shopping bag: Chinese characters, English, and Thai script. What I liked most about these businesses was that they had found a way to sidestep the seemingly irresistible onslaught of chain stores and franchises.

84

The convenience store and the supermarket were both far busier than the 7-Eleven which occupied a prime spot on the street. The operators of that store, restricted in what they could offer by their corporate master, were effectively ignoring many of their potential customers, and were paying the price.

*   *   *

Yungkang is to modern-day Taiwan what Bradford was to Victorian England. It lacks the sulfurous pall that used to hang over the cities of Yorkshire and Lancashire, however. Instead, the air in this industrial town is a gritty broth of vehicle fumes, factory emissions, and dust from construction sites.

Chungcheng South Road connects old Tainan with its upstart suburb. One thing only enlivens this bleak, perpetually congested thoroughfare: the "betel-nut beauties," micro-skirted teenage girls ensconced in brightly lit, glass-sided kiosks beside the road. These girls – dozens of them are stationed along the road – sell boxes of betel-nut, soft drinks and cigarettes to passing motorists. The prurient claim that some of them offer sexual services as a side-line. But if anything, the availability of this kind of work, which pays well and requires nothing more than a good figure and a willingness to wear skimpy clothes, has probably saved some high-school dropouts from prostitution.

In Yungkang, as in every city and town on the island, there are buildings that look like monuments to shoddiness. Those that are soundly constructed are seldom well maintained – externally at least. A great many homes and offices are luxuriously furnished and spotlessly clean on the inside, but have stained, discolored exteriors, and exist in neighborhoods where the sidewalks have been shattered by overloaded trucks; where plastic bags blow around like tumbleweeds; and where dog feces threaten the health of children playing outside. I have visited many countries: Nowhere has the gulf between private affluence and public squalor seemed so huge and so obvious as it is in Taiwan, and nowhere have I seen so many people who are fastidious about the state of their hair, clothes and homes behave so reprehensibly toward the environment.

Chinese people often attach upbeat names to the places they inhabit. Yungkang could reasonably be called prosperous, flourishing or booming. Incredibly though, the name of this noisome, dispiriting place translates as "eternal health."

HUNGRY GHOSTS AND HELL MARRIAGES

Taiwanese people seem to take the Festival of Hungry Ghosts a little more seriously than Britons and Americans do Halloween or Walpurgisnight.

Traditionally-minded Chinese believe that between the fifteenth day of the seventh lunar month and the fifteenth day of the eighth, the dead return to the world of the living. Throughout Ghost Month risky activities should be avoided. Fewer people go swimming or take airplanes; a great deal of non-urgent surgery is postponed. It is not a good idea to move house, marry, or open a new business during this period. Some people even drive less recklessly.

These precautions are necessary because some of the spirits abroad at that time are Hungry Ghosts – what the Taiwanese euphemistically refer to as "Good Brethren." These phantoms are jealous of the living, and considered dangerous enough to warrant propitiation. People attempt to placate these harassing specters with offerings of rice, fruit, ghost money and incense. Thousands of lanterns are set out to lead lonely ghosts to the feasts; still more are released on water to light the way for those who drowned.

Hungry Ghosts are the souls of people who have died, but whose existence in the next world is far from happy. They are stuck in the afterworld. They cannot be reborn until they find a living soul to take their place. For this reason, bodies of water where people are known to have drowned are judiciously avoided. The souls of those who died this way are said to linger in the water, and wait like kelpies for a chance to pull in a new victim.

Those who were murdered, executed, or otherwise died before their time are also likely to become Hungry Ghosts. The ghosts of suicides are especially feared on account of their tendency to wreak revenge on those they blame for their unhappiness. When a fatal road accident occurs, local residents sometimes rush out of their homes and burn ghost money amidst the human and vehicular wreckage to ensure that the spirits of those who were killed do not haunt the place where they died.

Living to a ripe old age and dying a peaceful death does not guarantee of a comfortable afterlife. Only male descendants and their spouses can perform the rituals of ancestor worship: Spirits who lack living male descendants will go unworshipped. No one burns ghost money for such beings, except during Ghost Month. Poverty and neglect will turn him or her into one of the wretched Good Brethren. This, according to Chinese tradition, is one of the most horrible fates imaginable. Consequently, the begetting of sons has been an absolute imperative for millennia.

The primary purpose of marriage was, until recently, to continue the bloodline. Even now matrimony does little to diminish the close relationship Chinese sons have with their parents. More than one married man told me that his mother – not his wife – was the most important person in his life.

It is still commonplace for the oldest son to bring his bride to live under the same roof as his parents. Chinese women are said to "marry out": They transfer allegiance from their biological parents to their in-laws. An American told me that this custom was why his Taiwanese wife had resolved to marry a foreigner long before meeting him. If she were to marry a Chinese man, she felt, she would not be able to keep up the close relationship she enjoyed with her mother.

Many men have found themselves torn between the duties they owe to their parents (obedience, care, and financial support), and the expectations of their wives and children. Even now it is the cause of many marriage break-ups. Sons who side with their parents at the expense of their own marital harmony are, according to classical thinking, acting admirably. The reasoning is simple: A man can replace his wife, but he can never find a new mother. In *Women And The Family In Rural Taiwan*, Margery Wolf writes: "It is well known that in times of crisis, sons are more dependable than husbands."

*   *   *

Having a male descendant is considered so vital that traditionalists are not above doing a little gerrymandering to ensure each man has at least one. If a male dies unmarried he may, at the instigation of his relatives, posthumously adopt a male child. This requires someone willing to donate a spare son for the purpose. The boy then makes ancestral sacrifices to his adoptive father; in every other respect he remains the legal son of his biological father.

This course of action can cause problems years later, however. One young woman, a high school teacher, told me about the situation in her family: "My uncle died when he was 24, so the younger of my two brothers was assigned to be his son. Right now my relatives consider my older brother to be my parents' only son, so there's a lot of pressure on him to get married. He's the only one who can continue the family line."

Producing a brood of daughters but no sons need not signal the end of a bloodline. If the father is wealthy and concerned about his lineage, he may make a pact with a prospective son-in-law. The father will provide his daughter with an attractive dowry, so long as it is understood that the first son to be born to the young couple will bear the family name of his maternal grandfather. In this way a gap in the bloodline can be bridged. Any subsequent sons will take their father's surname.

Siblings growing up together but bearing different family

names may seem odd and unsatisfactory. Some families, therefore, go one step further. They require their daughter's husband to "marry in" – live with his parents-in-law and, much more importantly, take his wife's father's family name. Any man who agrees to such terms may well be regarded as abandoning his own ancestors. He would also be tightly controlled by his in-laws: Their worry is that he might elope with their daughter, and return to his natal family. The most effective way of preventing this is to impress upon the son-in-law that he stands one day to inherit considerable property if he remains within the fold.

Even if a couple has no sons, are unable to adopt one, and are too poor to persuade a man to "marry in," all may not be lost. One of their daughters may remain single, take a lover, and give birth to illegitimate children. Those children will take their mother's maiden name – their maternal grandfather's surname. If among them there is a son, the lineage is saved. But Margery Wolf's assertion that "This technique for ensuring a descent line is not uncommon in Taiwan," seems extraordinary, and none of my informants said they had ever heard of such a thing happening, even in the distant past.

Wolf also writes that, if a married woman finds her husband is incapable of impregnating her, she may, possibly with the collusion of her mother-in-law, find another man to perform this task. Any progeny resulting from the liaison would, of course, be attributed to the husband.

In former times, a young widow who remained with her parents-in-law, abjuring remarriage, was regarded as especially virtuous. If she failed to produce a son during her husband's lifetime, but gave birth to one more than nine months after his demise, her stock – according to some writers – would actually rise. Ensuring the continuation of the family line would outweigh any sexual misdemeanors. The demands of lineage, ancestor worship and filial piety were once so monolithic as to overrule every other moral tenet.

*   *   *

Nothing illustrates the position of women in the traditional scheme better than the thousands-of-years-old practice of arranging weddings for females who have already died. These "hell marriages" (as the Chinese call them) almost certainly still occur in Taiwan. And despite communist efforts to stamp out religion and superstition, the custom is far from dead on the mainland.

In 1995, the 19-year-old daughter of a farmer in the mainland province of Shandong was murdered. After grieving, the farmer and his wife set about finding a match for the girl. This proved easier than expected. So many families wanted their sons to marry the dead girl that the farmer decided to hold an auction, with the participants representing families whose sons had died unmarried. The winning bid was the equivalent of more than US$2,000 – a fortune in rural China.

More hell marriages came to light the following year. In Shaanxi province two brothers-in-law were arrested and charged with digging up and selling the remains of two women. The female corpses had been bought by the relatives of two men who had died unmarried, so that they could be wedded to and buried with those men.

The Chinese have long believed that men are prone to loneliness in the next world if they have no women to attend to them. In the very distant past wives and concubines were put to death when their husbands died. A form of suttee replaced this practice, with officials of the imperial government sometimes eulogizing widows who committed suicide when their husbands died.

But if a boy died before marrying, there was only one way in which his relatives could ensure his eternal happiness: by arranging a post-mortal wedding. These even occurred in China's imperial family, and sometimes involved infants who had died before their first birthday.

According to a news report, the Shandong girl and the young man whose family won the auction were posthumously united so that both would have somebody to accompany them in the afterlife. Not all ghost weddings are arranged out of compassion for the deceased, however. In David K. Jordan's excellent elucidation of Taiwanese folk religion *Gods, Ghosts And Ancestors*, he discusses a case in which a man married both of his wife's younger sisters because: "About a year before the ghost wedding [the man's wife] became subject to periods of illness characterized by weariness and aches. Western medicine, the family maintained, did not seem to help her, and although she never considered herself to be especially religious, she was persuaded by friends and neighbors to consult an oracle."

The oracle announced that the woman was sick because spirits in her home wanted to marry her husband. The couple's initial reaction was disbelief, but a second divination session confirmed that a ghost wedding was necessary. Marriage rites were then arranged, with paper-and-cloth dummies taking the place of a living bride. When the wedding was over the two mannequins were burned in order to send the troublesome spirits back to the supernatural world.

Given the relative unimportance of daughters in traditional Chinese society, it seems odd that Taiwanese ghost weddings are usually arranged to satisfy female spirits. In *The Cult Of The Dead In A Chinese Village*, Emily Martin Ahern, who like Jordan did her fieldwork in Taiwan, explains: "[If a girl] dies before being transferred to her husband's lineage, it is felt that she has been caught in the wrong place. She has no right at all to care or worship from the members of her natal lineage. She was born to leave it."

Deceased maiden daughters are therefore considered anomalous, probably shameful, and quite possibly inauspicious.

Such females are buried in simple graves. Their ancestral tablets cannot be placed on the altar in their parents' home: instead they must be hidden somewhere in the house, or put in a special temple for unmarried girls. The sentiment that a woman without a husband is in some way incomplete is still widespread: Unmarried females over the age of thirty are often the subject of both pity and pressure.

Jordan describes the unusual way in which men are sometimes recruited to take part in ghost weddings: "A groom is found by the family laying 'bait' in the middle of a road. This usually takes the form of a red envelope (used in China for gifts of money). A passer-by sooner or later picks up the envelope, and immediately the family of the spirit come out of hiding beside the road and announce to the young man that he is the chosen bridegroom. If he refuses, he is of course in danger of vengeance by the ghost…"

Such sleight is not always necessary. A volunteer will come forward if the girl's family offers an attractive dowry. The ghost's bridegroom can use this money to pay the bride price when he later marries for real. It is said that some men are actually eager to marry a ghost, believing that such a wife can give them good *guanxi* (a network of relationships) in the afterworld.

Jordan came across two hell marriages in the village where he spent a year and a half in the late 1960s. He believes there could have been more, but found that people tended not to volunteer information about such shameful episodes.

My own efforts to uncover ghost weddings suggested such rituals were a thing of the past. I asked students and friends if they had ever witnessed such an event. None had. But my wife, who grew up in a small village in Tainan County, recalled her neighbors arranging a ghost wedding in the early 1980s.

Then at the end of 1999, the English-language press reported two posthumous marriages. The first united a man with his fiancée, a teacher who had died in the massive September 21 earthquake. After giving up any hope that the young woman might have survived the disaster, the man was visited in his dreams by his sweetheart, who reminded him of his promise to marry her come what may. A photographer retouched some old photos so the deceased could appear at the ceremony in a bridal outfit. The bridegroom carried his ghost wife's ancestral tablet into his home at the conclusion of the wedding, and was quoted as saying: "I have married her despite her death and I will not regret this as long as I live."

The second ghost marriage concerned a man surnamed Chang and his late girlfriend, whose family name was Tsai. They wed twenty years after their original marriage plans had been thwarted by his parents. Tsai, pregnant with her boyfriend's child, had committed suicide, while Chang had gone onto marry a woman acceptable to his parents. Tsai's sisters said their dead sibling had often visited them in dreams and expressed her desire to get married. At the urging of an elder at the temple where Tsai's remains were kept, Chang finally went ahead with the long-delayed wedding.

*   *   *

Marrying a ghost is not the only intriguing matrimonial possibility in Taiwan. The incest taboo does not extend to informally adopted siblings. It is possible for a girl to wed her foster brother.

Before World War II it was standard practice in certain parts of the island, including some aboriginal districts, to exchange biological daughters for foster daughters. This was done at a very young age. It suited both families: the girl's biological parents would not have to waste money on a child destined to leave them; the foster parents could train the girl in whatever skills they hoped to see in their daughter-in-law. Fifteen or twenty years later the foster daughter would wed the biological son of her adoptive parents.

The custom began to die out when industrialization gave young people enough economic independence to defy their parents. Still, there must be hundreds if not thousands of septuagenarian and octogenarian couples alive today who were betrothed as infants, and who cannot remember a time when they were not living together.

CINEMA OF THE GODS

Chinese gods seem to have a taste for violent and risqué films. The spirits enshrined at the temple nearest my first home in Tainan had a particular liking for Hong Kong kung fu movies. On auspicious days the temple's management committee would set up a projector at one end of the car park and a screen at the other. This entertainment was put on for the deities, but anyone from the neighborhood could enjoy it. Like the kids who sat and watched from the temple's front steps, I appreciated these shows, and the fact that they were always free: There was neither a donation box nor a collection plate.

Being hemmed in on three sides by tall buildings did not stop another, much smaller temple from also laying on movies. The projector sat under the eaves of the shrine – which was smaller than a mom-and-pop store – while the screen was positioned on the other side of a busy thoroughfare. The sound level was usually set so high that all traffic noise was drowned out. Those who lingered suffered sensory overload; for passing drivers the screenings must have been a dangerous distraction.

*   *   *

Dedicated to Taiwan's most popular deity – Matsu, the Queen of Heaven and the protector of fishermen and sailors – Taichung's Wanchungong is in many respects a typical temple.

There has been a shrine on this site since 1722, but the current structure was built after World War II. I visited it early on a weekday morning, and found myself among senior citizens, housewives – and smartly-attired office ladies sacrificing incense before work. By the main entrance, hawkers sold spirit money, while a monk, a nun and a crippled beggar competed for alms. Cookies, crackers, fruits, corn chips, cans of soda and oolong tea were spread out over two large offertory tables.

Worshipers tossed bundles of mock currency into the temple's spirit-money furnaces. Fortunately for those living in the neighborhood, mounted on the top of each furnace's smokestack was a device which sprayed water through the rising air. This contrivance, it was obvious, was designed to prevent large particles of soot from being released into the city's already polluted atmosphere.

Seeing this pleased me. It also made me wonder just what prevents other temples from utilizing this simple but effective technology. I have visited hundreds of places of worship in Taiwan. In a few, the practice of burning spirit money has been abolished. But Taichung's Wanchungong is the only one where I have seen air scrubbers installed.

*   *   *

Just as the UK has so-called animal lovers who eat meat almost every day, Taiwan surely has people who oppose trash incinerators, yet burn spirit money on the first and fifteenth day of every lunar month, during Ghost Month, and on the birthdays of deceased relatives.

This practice may not be entirely pointless. One of my students argued it is a way for people to release their sorrow, and overcome a feeling that they did not do enough for the deceased when he or she was alive. But seeing the vast quantities of spirit money which Taiwanese people burn, I sometimes wondered if the afterworld was not in danger of suffering a bout of hyper-inflation similar to that which contributed to the KMT's defeat in mainland China.

*　　　　　*　　　　　*

Nothing documents the half-hearted adoption of Occidental ways better than the calendars which hang in every home and factory. Beneath bold Gregorian numerals, small Chinese ideograms indicate the lunar date. Shopkeepers require this information if they are to follow tradition and propitiate the spirit world on the first and fifteenth day of each lunar month, while part-time vegetarians need to know when they can and cannot eat meat.

Most weddings and business launches are planned only after a fortune teller, or at least an almanac, has been consulted. And when I opened an account at a local financial institution, I was invited to select the account's number. The clerk explained that the bank dared not risk losing a new client by foisting a potentially inauspicious number on him or her, and so allowed every customer to choose from a list of unassigned numbers.

*　　　　　*　　　　　*

Several indigenous faiths have appeared in recent years. One of the best known is the UFO cult which migrated en masse to Texas in 1998. This group, which called itself God's Salvation Church, was led by Dr. Chen Heng-ming, a former professor. Chen claimed to have fathered Jesus 2,000 years ago, and to talk to God through a ring on his finger. He led 200 followers to a Dallas suburb where he prophesied that God would appear – first on their television sets, then in person, arriving by flying saucer. The sect members constructed a "spaceship" from tires and plywood. Like Buddhists, they stocked their shrine with fruit, soda and crackers. When God failed to show up, Chen's reaction was admirably candid. "My predictions can be considered nonsense," he is reported to have said.

Chen seems to have meant well. Other cult leaders, however, have been more interested in accumulating cash than in enlightening their followers. In recent years, several false gurus and mystics have persuaded the credulous to part with millions of NT dollars. "There seem to be more and more religions, but less and less peace, hope, love and joy," an American Protestant missionary told me.

Social scientists and commentators have speculated as to why Taiwan is such a fertile breeding ground for bizarre sects. In 1998, then Justice Minister Mr. Liao Cheng-hao offered one explanation: "Our economy has grown very fast. People have money, but have not developed mentally at the same speed. They feel empty and grab hold of religion. It is very easy for fake creeds to steal their money."

*   *   *

Around public telephones and in pedestrian subways – where in Britain people expect to see senseless graffiti, or adverts for prostitutes – I often found stacks of Buddhist pamphlets.

One bilingual booklet entitled "The Law of Causality" warned that people who scold beggars are likely to "starve to death at the road side." Fathers who do not love their children risk becoming lonely widowers; young men who violate the daughters of others are destined never to marry. Those who are jealous by nature will develop a bad body odor, and those who feel happy when seeing others endure misfortune are liable to suffer constant sickness.

*   *   *

When I was working at a kindergarten – a pleasant, well-paid job that consisted mainly of teaching doggerel to young children – one task at the beginning of each semester was to confer English names on any boys and girls who lacked them. I always tried to find names that were easy to write and pronounce, but a little unusual and so easier to remember.

Once I named a boy Ian. This satisfied both my Taiwanese co-teacher and the four-year-old in question. Nevertheless, the next day I was told that I would have to rename him: His parents had found my choice disturbing. The problem was that "Ian" has a similar pronunciation to the Mandarin word for hospital, *yi-yuan.*

*   *   *

The traditionally-minded believe that the spirit of a dead person may haunt the spot where he or she died. This makes hospitals especially hazardous places, and is why many doctors and nurses wear Taoist amulets. If a man dies in some far off place, his relatives may conduct special rituals to call his soul home. Also, because of these notions, ambulances are sometimes mobilized to take hospital patients who are very near death back to their families. Some patients, of course, expire en route. In such cases the accompanying doctor will usually not pronounce death until after his charge has arrived – a fiction intended to console the family of the deceased.

*   *   *

Some Tainan acquaintances told me that from time to time, they would withdraw to a temple for the weekend. None of them were fervent Buddhists, though some of them had been encouraged to join these activities by pious relatives or friends. Most regarded these retreats as Westerners might a visit to a health farm: a temporary escape from the stress, pollution and temptations of big-city life.

One young woman told me that she had returned to the same nunnery more than two dozen times. The sheer peacefulness of the place pulled her back again and again, she explained.

Another, a bank worker who sometimes visited a monastic community in central Taiwan, thought that such retreats have minimal spiritual value. "If you feel frustrated or have some trouble in your life, [staying in a temple] for a day or two can help you forget your problems, but it won't solve them," she said. "I've found that the monks and nuns don't give any really effective advice. Usually they just say something like: 'Calm down. It's just a phase, it'll pass.' If you're being mistreated by your boss or your husband, they'll say that it may well be because of sins you committed in a previous life. He or she is hurting you because, in a previous existence, you did something bad to that person. It's a debt you have to repay. You shouldn't fight back or retaliate: You should accept these troubles, then everything will balance out…"

But after spending time with monks and nuns, she had a great deal of respect for those who opt for a monastic existence: "It's not an easy life. It's not an escape from reality. They don't eat for enjoyment – they eat only to sustain their bodies. And they have to follow a lot of rules."

Certain monasteries did indeed sound strict. In some, even paying guests are required to wear garments similar to monks' and nuns' habits; attendance at pre-breakfast (meaning pre-dawn) rituals is compulsory; meals are eaten in silence, with men and women seated separately, and every scrap of food must be consumed. However, my interest was piqued, so one Sunday I set off for Lion's Head Mountain, a popular retreat on the boundary of Hsinchu and Miaoli counties.

On arriving I found a car park overflowing with tour buses, and the whole area teeming with people. Many did not stray far from the souvenir shops. Nevertheless, every trail, pavilion and vantage point seemed to be occupied by families or clusters of old people. I saw one woman, oblivious or insensitive to Buddhist dietary injunctions, hand strips of beef jerky to three ravenous children.

The mountainside is dotted with shrines and monasteries, and it took me a while to locate the hall where I had made a reservation. I checked in, and wandered around the dormitory. It adjoined a sizable temple, but felt like an ordinary hostel – only more dilapidated.

Dinnertime came soon after sunset. The other lay visitors and I did not eat with the monks and nuns, but with the janitors. The vegetarian fare was tasty, but hardly consumed in contemplative silence: people chatted, and infants ran pell-mell around the canteen.

Afterward there was little to do except take a stroll. The day-trippers had disappeared; finally, Lion's Head Mountain was blissfully quiet. The air was cool and clean, and the lights of the nearest town were reassuringly distant. The silhouettes of the various temples gave the hillside a timeless air, but the atmosphere was hardly hallowed. Off-duty monks and nuns watched TV or read newspapers; beer was available from vending machines.

I retired early, and slept soundly until votive drums and gongs shook me awake at 4:40 a.m. I spent a while watching the monks as they chanted and prayed, and noticed that the others guests did not even do this.

After breakfast – in food and mood, dinner reprised – I packed my things and left, and hiked down the hill toward a major road. The scenery was lovely, and the environment restful, but I immediately realized that in psychic terms the place had made far less of an impression on me than Taiwan's high mountains. But I had expected no epiphanies, and so did not leave disappointed.

*   *   *

In the southwest there is an exceptionally beautiful valley deep in the mountains called Sanmin. This is a curious name for a local government division: Sanmin is a shortened form of *San Min Chu Yi* – the Three Principles of the People, the official ideology of the Republic of China. The three major settlements located in the valley – villages, not towns – are each named after one of Dr. Sun Yat-sen's Three Principles: *Mintsu* (meaning "national-ism"), *Minchuan* ("democracy") and *Minsheng* ("the people's livelihood"). Together these mean, roughly, "of the people, by the people, for the people."

An evangelical Christian sect called the New Testament Church has settled part of the valley. The church was founded by a Hong Kong woman known to her followers as Sister Kung. When she died in 1966, the leadership passed to Mr. Elijah Han, a native of Tainan County. Han had a revelation from God that a Christian community should be established on a mountainside in Sanmin. The faithful soon set to work, and now more than a hundred people live permanently on the site. The community has come into conflict with the authorities over land use, and they have agitated for the right to educate their children by themselves. Some Taiwanese regard them as pseudo-communists and eccentrics.

*   *   *

Religious conflict of any sort is extremely rare in Taiwan, but I did hear of one case in which a Christian girl was unable to marry her non-Christian boyfriend because of religious differences with her prospective parents-in-law. The boy's family was very traditional, and informed the girl that after marriage she would have to fulfill all the duties of a Chinese daughter-in-law. She had no objection to living with and submitting to the boy's parents: the sticking point was ancestor worship. When she made it clear that she would pray to no entity except God, her relationship with the boy came to an abrupt end.

*   *   *

I am not a churchgoer, but I admire the social and educational contributions foreign Christian missionaries have made to Taiwan, and have met some of the 2,000 or so active in the ROC. One of the most remarkable is Father Peter Mertens, a Belgian Catholic who has spent almost half a century in Taiwan, and seen his share of history.

In 1954, Mertens joined crowds greeting Communist Chinese POWs who, after being captured during the Korean War, opted to begin new lives in Taiwan, rather than return to the mainland. In the 1970s he organized relief efforts for Vietnamese "boat people" appearing in the waters around Taiwan. He has also served as a parish priest, and when I met him in late 2000, he was executive secretary of the Bishops' Commission for Social Development, and running the Taiwan branch of the charity Caritas.

I was impressed by the warmth of Sister Dorothy Folmer – an American nun who has worked in orphanages, old people's homes, a hospice for the terminally ill, and now spends much of her time providing moral and practical support for AIDS victims and their families, in hospitals, prisons, and patients' homes.

Since first arriving in 1984, American Baptist church planter Robert Burris has witnessed great social changes, many of them for the worse. "The family structure is breaking down… drug use and promiscuity are increasing, while traditional filial piety is in decline," he said, but stressed that "the Taiwanese remain so very kind to us, and are indeed a warmhearted people." Another Protestant shared his insights on the development of Christianity in Taiwan. David Alexander, who has worked with

Taiwan's Presbyterian Church for more than 20 years, said: "You can't pass the Gospel out with relief goods as was done in the fifties, or by providing social services, like in the sixties and seventies. Now the Gospel has to stand on its own merit, and that of the people who attempt to live it," he told me.

Political reform seems to have made Alexander's work easier. During the martial law era, the Presbyterian Church – particularly in south Taiwan – was a locus of political dissent. During the early 1980s, foreigners working for other churches had "missionary" written on their ID documents, but those belonging to the Presbyterian Church had "Presbyterian" marked on their cards.

"It was as good as a red flag," Alexander said. "I was monitored by the police and military." Nowadays, he said, he is greeted warmly whenever he goes to government offices – even after delivering a speech at a pro-independence rally.

*   *   *

Missionaries operated under difficult conditions during the Japanese occupation, but since World War II they have had a free hand. In this respect, few Asian governments are as accommodating as the ROC's. However, Christianity has so far failed to displace local religions. Most temples appear to be thriving: I have yet to come across a Buddhist or Taoist place of worship that has been deconsecrated.

Evangelists appreciate the difficulty of what they are attempting. According to one church group's Web site: "Funerals are thoroughly pagan and saturated with the fear of death and of ghosts. Reports of demonic possession are not an uncommon occurrence. It is the consensus of evangelical missionaries in Taiwan that Satan has a stranglehold on this island. These people are as lost intellectually and spiritually as a people can be."

After more than 350 years of proselytizing, no more than

seven percent of Taiwan's population has been baptized. This suggests that mainland China has little to fear from foreign missionaries.

*　　　　*　　　　*

Protestant churches in Taiwan tend to resemble their counterparts in North America or Europe, or else look like small office buildings. Many Catholic churches, however, have been constructed in the style of Chinese temples: green and red tiles, curling eaves and vermilion columns.

Father Peter Mertens linked this to the Catholic Church's desire to stress that converting to Christianity does not mean ceasing to be Chinese. The number of Catholics in the ROC has scarcely risen since the early 1960s, however, whereas the number of Protestants has increased substantially – despite the evangelicals' staunch opposition to ancestor worship. (The Catholic Church stipulates that its followers should not burn spirit money for their forefathers, but allows them to offer incense, wine, fruit or flowers.)

*　　　　*　　　　*

Ask a Taiwanese person what his surname is, and very likely he will answer Lee, Chen or Chang. A local proverb holds that, "Chen, Lin, Lee, Kuo and Tsai are half the people in the world." This is not such a great exaggeration: If the list is expanded to eleven names by adding Huang, Chang, Wang, Wu, Yang and Liu, over half the house-holds on the island are accounted for.

Chinese society does not lack family names as such: There are perhaps 800 different ones in Taiwan, and thousands more on the mainland, which is ethnically far more diverse. But it does differ from most Western societies insofar as a very small number of surnames make up a huge proportion of the population. This situation has come about for a number of reasons. The Chinese have been using family names longer than almost any other civilization on Earth. The "evolutionary dwindling" of surnames which occurs worldwide, as less common ones die out, has therefore been especially acute. During periods of clan warfare, weak surname groups were often subsumed en masse by stronger clans. Many of Taiwan's aborigines still use Han Chinese surnames.

A person's family name used to be of critical importance when he or she came to marry. The rule of surname exogamy – that no man could marry a woman whose family name was identical to his – stemmed from an ancient belief that all people sharing the same surname are necessarily blood relatives.

This rule applied even when the two parties came from different provinces. The written form of the surname was all important – its pronunciation did not matter. A Mandarin-speaker called Wu was therefore barred from marrying a Cantonese-speaker who pronounced his name Ng.

The legal code of the Qing Dynasty stated that all identical-surname marriages were null and void, that both parties should receive sixty blows of a club, and that all wedding presents be forfeited to the government.

In both the ROC and the PRC people are no longer bound by the principle of surname exogamy. However, those who insist on marrying within their surname group sometimes face residual prejudice, particularly in rural areas.

*   *   *

Many Taiwanese youths curse in English. Some think it is cool and fashionable, while others do it, I was told, because they think that those around them will be impressed by their grasp of the language.

I dislike this habit, largely because it strikes me as epitomizing one of the defects of Taiwanese culture – the tendency to indiscriminately adopt Western ideas and behavior, even when it is unnecessary (such as substituting Valentine's Day for Chinese Lovers' Day), not suited to Taiwan (mass car ownership), or just downright idiotic (English-language cursing falls into this category). However, I cannot blame those youngsters. Foul-mouthed performers are a staple of the West's cultural exports, from which there is no escaping.

*   *   *

Less than an hour of daylight remained; another trip to the mountains was almost over. I began soliciting lifts, and soon found myself in a small pickup driven by an aboriginal man.

As we sped over an unsurfaced stretch of road, I described to him how I had spent the day. He asked me the several questions. I was the first foreigner he had met who was not a church worker.

"Do you like Taiwan?" he asked me.

"Yes, I like the high mountains. Britain's tallest mountain is not much higher than Yangmingshan…"

"Britain is flat?" The realization seemed to strike a chord with him. After a few seconds' mulling this intelligence, he spoke portentously, as if he had just divined the reason for my country's erstwhile greatness: "Britain's land must be very good for growing rice."

BLOOD AND RITUAL

The blowtorch had failed to ignite the sheaves of spirit money, so the master of ceremonies splashed kerosene over the sodden pile and put a cigarette to it. Flames leapt up briefly, but the heaviness of the spring rain was such that the fire was soon quenched. Unconcerned, the man turned his attention to another stack of currency for the gods, doused and lit it...

Behind him a shirtless and sword-wielding *tang-ki* (as spirit mediums are called in the Taiwanese language) lurched from one steaming heap of mock money to the next. Only his apron – a colorful embroidery of supernatural symbols – marked him out as a divine intermediary, not a lunatic running amok. Each time the medium stopped, he applied the blade to his body. Splashes of blood flowered momentarily on his shoulders and back before disappearing in rivulets of rainwater. The devout believe that such men are possessed, and protected from injury, by their gods. In his trance-like state, this medium seemed oblivious to both pain and the weather.

A clutch of firecrackers exploded, adding yet more smoke to the hazy atmosphere. Their acrid mustiness made me cough. The firecrackers were deafening, but it was the constant amplified drumming that I felt would stave my head in. The drum was three meters across and occupied the back of a small truck. Around it stood four young women dressed in mustard tracksuits. Their thunderous beating was constant and practiced. Taiwanese pilgrims often resemble teams of athletes, and seem to train just as hard.

A steward ran back and forth among the spectators, his face reddened by the bluster needed to make his whistle audible above the din. He was trying, with little success, to keep onlookers a safe distance from the spirit medium. Despite smoldering ash underfoot and a dangerous weapon being swung in random arcs about our heads, we all seemed compelled to move closer to the *tang-ki*. Perhaps it was for safety's sake that the Japanese colonial authorities had outlawed possession.

We had traveled north across a flat landscape of fish farms and salt ponds to see this gruesome spectacle. Nankunshen Temple is renowned for its noisy and bloody rituals. It hosts a commingling of creeds, a melange of Buddhism, Taoism, folk beliefs and local legends.

Hsin-yi and Mei-ling explained this to me with informed indifference: Both grew up in the bastion of tradition that is Tainan, but both are Christian. While waiting in the bus station they had translated for me a triptych of sorts: Adverts for vehicle insurance and gas stoves flanked a short political slogan, a hangover from the era of Nationalist dictatorship. The size of the motto made it easy to overlook. It seemed to be there to remind, rather than foment:

THREE PRINCIPLES OF THE PEOPLE
SHALL REUNIFY CHINA

The author of the Three Principles, Dr. Sun Yat-sen, was a Christian. So were Generalissimo and Madame Chiang Kai-shek. Yet ancient traditions have survived better in the Nationalist domain than anywhere else in the Chinese world. On the mainland many customs and practices have been extirpated by the Communists. And compared to the riotous goings-on in Taiwanese temples, Chinese religion in Hong Kong and Singapore is a somber, sanitized affair.

Nankunshen Temple is an ornate structure, yet few notice the antique carvings and paintings which adorn the interior. The Five Kings enshrined here hold lofty positions in the hierarchy of gods. But only a minority of visitors petition this powerful quintet. Most people (and on festival days there are thousands) come to witness the ataxic movements and self-mutilation of the *tang-ki*.

These grisly and mesmerizing displays are peripheral – bloody sideshows demonstrating the protective power of the deities being celebrated. It is the weekly convergence of gods that makes Nankunshen important. Every Sunday, pilgrims from all over Taiwan bring icons of their local divinities here. Sunday has no special significance in the Chinese almanac. Nowadays Chinese folk religion is practiced mainly on the Christian Sabbath, simply because then the faithful need not go to work.

Worshippers arriving with a god in tow hope that the pilgrimage can fortify and invigorate their patron. At the heart of Chinese religion lies a frank reciprocity: Supernatural entities must bring good fortune to their followers, or suffer abandonment. Statues of disappointing gods, or tablets representing unhelpful ancestors, are sometimes smashed and dumped without ceremony.

A few yards behind the advancing spirit medium, four men carried a palanquin bearing the wood-and-cloth effigy of a god. They bounced the roofed litter up and down over each half-burnt, half-sodden pile of votive money, then, like skilled pallbearers, turned ninety degrees on the spot. Their progress towards the temple was a slow zigzag. We left them and sought shelter inside.

There are several altars in the temple, each one unique in appearance and dedication. A Taoist priest in red and black robes stood before one sooty clutter of icons and bellowed an incantation. Hsin-yi confessed that his words were so arcane, his intonation so odd, that she could understand almost nothing, despite being an everyday speaker of Taiwanese. It is said that some clerics purposely encrypt their litanies so as to preserve a monopoly over certain lucrative rites.

Another group of celebrants entered the temple. Their vanguard consisted of five *tang-ki*. Two of them looked to be past retirement age – short gray-haired men whose thin bodies suggested protein-deficient childhoods. The youngest was pot-bellied and pale-skinned. Blood ran from just beneath his ruffled fringe, down his hairless chest and over his stomach. His eyes shone with a degree of conviction that his companions seemed to lack.

At the appropriate moment the five cut themselves once again. The pot-bellied youth dragged a mace down his forehead and over his nose and lips. His mouth hung open, his tongue resting on a lacerated lower lip. I began to wonder if he was mentally lacking: On a previous visit to Nankunshen I had come across a crew made up entirely, it seemed, of retardates. A Norwegian missionary named Reichelt, writing in the 1950s, alleged that vulnerable people are sometimes pressured into becoming spirit mediums. He wrote: "It is especially the young, highly-strung boys, whose nervous and emotional organization is easily affected, who are used in this sinister and repellent traffic." In 1998, *The China Post* reported that certain unscrupulous temples were, "luring young vagabonds to make money for them by posing as fakirs and performing dangerous feats to make people believe they are messengers of gods."

The self-mutilating having ceased for a minute, a man stepped out of the crowd and began sponging the mediums down as if they were boxers resting between the rounds of a fight. Near him a middle-aged woman stood nursing a trolley full of swords, axes and other weapons – the team's caddie.

An instrument I had not seen before came into play: a bright scarlet sphere, about the size of a tennis ball, from which several spikes protruded. The Taiwanese call this fearsome object a "heavenly red tangerine." One of the tang-ki held it in his hand as if gauging its weight, then threw it upward. The spiky ball fell back to Earth; the medium lent forward so that it bounced off his scalp. Like a soccer player honing his heading skills, he casually repeated the action several times. Throughout his face was a model of transcendent inscrutability.

Escaping from the crush, I stepped outside to find that it had stopped raining. Yet another deity was making its final approach to the temple, led by two *tang-ki*. They were both lean, brown-skinned young men. In addition to having cut themselves in the conventional manner, long needles perforated the faces and arms of both men: two through the cheeks, one above and one below each elbow. When the procession stopped, both mediums trembled for several seconds, building up to the instant when they would again mortify their flesh.

Mei-ling and Hsin-yi had disappeared. They were driven away, they told me later, by hunger rather than horror, and took refuge among some snack stalls. Such heathen shenanigans as self-mutilation bored them, they declared. Both had seen such things several times before. Then, with a glee that belied her professed disinterest, Mei-ling described a bloody episode she had witnessed as a teenager.

Alone I followed the two young mediums until their activities for the afternoon were completed. In the temple's car park I discovered that what happens when the lacerating and gashing has finished is, if anything, more shocking than blood-spilling itself.

The two *tang-ki* were disarmed. A practitioner of folk medicine sauntered over, discarded his cigarette, and uncapped a bottle of liquor. This he held to the lips of each medium before taking a swig himself. The alcohol no doubt fortified the *tang-ki*. But the medicine man did not swallow his. After plucking the needles from the cheeks and elbows of the mediums, he spat and dribbled wine over their wounds. Then he took a sheet of ghost money he had previously tucked into his belt, wrote an invisible spell on it with the tip of his finger, and rubbed it over each patch of broken skin. This concluded the treatment. Shamans are convinced that their gods protect them from infection as well as pain. The faithful assert that the wounds they incur heal abnormally fast.

An action resembling the Heimlich maneuver was used to expel the possessing spirits. The deprogrammer gripped one of the mediums around the waist from behind, and lifted him clean off his feet. The *tang-ki* threw his arms into the air and flailed weakly. He was lowered gently to the ground and lay limp for a few moments. The procedure was then repeated with the other medium. A few minutes later, both men walked away as if nothing untoward had happened.

I too walked away, and sat in one of those small pavilions that can be found in parks and public places throughout the Chinese world. Usually my curiosity is insatiable, but for once I had seen enough. I brooded until Hsin-yi and Mei-ling returned. The day had been absorbing. Nevertheless, it seemed to underline the difficulties I was having taking measure of this society. I had read that one of the most fundamental duties a Chinese son owes to his parents is to preserve and protect his own body – "He who abuses his body outrages and wounds his parents." And yet I had seen self-mortification condoned when it occurred in a religious context, and had heard non-believers speak of it highly as a form of entertainment. No rule in Taiwan, it appears, is hard and fast.

THE UNITY WAY

Thirty kilometers east of Tainan, a huge temple overlooks a small village. Precious Radiance Temple so dominates the hamlet of Yushan* that passers-by could be forgiven for assuming the shrine was built first, and that it inspired people to settle in its shadow. In fact, this sprawling complex of worship halls, classrooms and columbaria is less than 30 years old.

What whetted my appetite to visit was learning that Precious Radiance belongs to one of Taiwan's more unusual creeds – a sect whose history of initial persecution, later acceptance and current popularity parallels that of Mormonism in the United States. I Kuan Tao, "the unity way," was founded in mainland China in 1928. By the time of the Communist takeover it had spread to every province. Many believers fled to Taiwan, but there they found themselves harassed and under police surveillance.

As soon as the sect formally re-established itself it was proscribed. The Nationalist regime was alarmed by similarities between I Kuan Tao and the anti-Qing secret societies which had proliferated in China before the revolution of 1911. Prudish KMT leaders were further perturbed by rumors that sect members worshipped in the nude. This was untrue, but I Kuan Tao doctrine blocked the faithful from refuting these allegations: Upon initiation converts swear an oath not to reveal details of the sect's

---

*The village's name is identical to that of Taiwan's highest mountain, but lies some distance away.

rites to non-members. Breaking this oath, it is said, jeopardizes the happy afterlife which the religion promises initiates.

Work on Precious Radiance Temple began the year after Chiang Kai-shek passed away. His death brought about an easing of repression, but the formal ban on I Kuan Tao was not lifted until 1987. Since then the group has come a long way. It claims two million initiates in Taiwan and thousands more overseas. Hundreds of temples have been built. The sect owns publishing houses, hospitals, and nursing homes.

The main hall of the temple looks, from a distance, not dissimilar to other places of worship in the Chinese world: a tiled roof, curling eaves and high columns. But its scale and coloring – gold and red – endow it with a quality few other Chinese temples have: a grandeur comparable to that of a fine European cathedral.

The car park in front of the temple suggests that the sect receives, or at least hopes for, many visitors indeed. But when I arrived just a few cars were parked there; the whole place seemed extremely quiet. There were no gongs, no drums, no firecrackers – none of the cacophony great temples usually generate. The only man-made sound was that of a lone workman hammering marble. I wondered if this lack of festive noise explained the lack of visitors: There seemed to be none of the joyful bedlam which draws crowds to religious centers such as Nankunshen.

It was difficult to tell which of the subsidiary buildings were for religious use and which had a practical function. I peered into storerooms and discovered a vegetarian canteen (the sect espouses strict vegetarianism). Several flights of stairs took me higher up the hillside until, just in front of the main hall, I emerged onto a marble platform large enough to host a football game. From its lip the view was enchanting: The rustic brick houses, the mango orchards, and the surrounding viridescent hills interwove as if they had been created to complement one another. Turning my attention to the hall, I noticed shoe-racks beside the two doorways. These are a standard feature of Japanese temples and Taiwanese homes, but this was the first shrine in Taiwan I had been to where visitors were expected to take their shoes off.

Bernard Newman, who traveled through Taiwan in 1960 and devoted a third of his book *Far Eastern Journey* to the island, thought that Westerners would perhaps regard Taoism more highly if its places of worship were at least kept clean. He would have liked Precious Radiance Temple: I Kuan Taoists obviously regard cleanliness as being next to Godliness. The interior of the main hall was spotless and uncluttered: members of the sect burn neither spirit money nor incense. The main altar bore flowers and offerings of fruit, but was free of the usual soot and grime. The statues on either side resembled those in other temples, but being spotless they seemed altogether more benign.

I Kuan Tao is an attempt to identify the common principles which underlie the world's great religions, a synthesis like Cao Dai, the Vietnamese concoction which attracted Graeme Greene. The reconciliation which I Kuan Tao claims to have achieved is expressed in the design and decoration of the main hall at Precious Radiance. In the center of the ceiling – around the yin and yang sign – are paintings which depict eight different belief systems. One panel represents Taoism, another Buddhism. Confucius and Mencius are pictured together. Christianity, Islam and Hinduism each warrant their own panels. The two remaining segments depict Wen Wang, author of the *I Ching* (*The Book of Changes*), and Fu Hsi, the mythical Emperor who is said to have discovered the original eight trigrams on the shell of a tortoise five millennia ago.

All this was explained to me by a uniformed attendant, a young woman who looked more like an airline stewardess than an adherent of a not-quite-mainstream religion. As she spoke a local tour group filed into the hall. Despite the sect's claims to have attracted a huge number of followers, and in spite of the physical evidence this great edifice constitutes, I had the feeling that most of the visitors that day were non-believers. We wandered around Precious Radiance Temple like the Japanese backpackers I had seen years before in St. Peter's Basilica: impressed by the scale and beauty of the place, but perplexed by or indifferent to the faith in whose name it had been created.

HEAD-HUNTERS AND CANNIBALS

Like Native Americans and Australian aborigines, Taiwan's indigenous people have become an impoverished minority in their own land. The life expectancy of aborigines is around fifteen years lower than the island's average; a disproportionate number die of alcoholism or in accidents. Despite affirmative action in education and government employment, relatively few members of the indigenous tribes go to university or enter the professions, and their unemployment rate is three times the national average. They are currently well represented in the fields of sport and pop music, but much of their culture has already been lost.

I was told by some Han Taiwanese that aborigines are poor because they like to drink, and are lazy (from what I have seen, the former is undoubtedly true, the latter nothing but an outright slur). For the same reasons, they said, a large number of aboriginal women are sold into the sex industry. It seems there are villages where young girls are one of the main cash crops. But none of my informants were able explain to me why Taiwan society needs so many prostitutes – around 100,000, the Taipei Times reported in April 2000 – or why so many of them (50,000 according to the Garden of Hope Foundation) are children.

The pitiful state of the mountain aborigines (the lowland tribes have almost completely assimilated into Han society) is due in large part to the remoteness of their villages. The gulf between Taiwan's cities and the island's countryside in terms of wealth, facilities and opportunities is wide, and also impedes the progress of Han Taiwanese in rural areas.

Aboriginal leaders have rightly lambasted the government's policy of importing Southeast Asian laborers while so many indigenous people are out of work. But business interests are powerful, and the advent of democracy has done little to help the aborigines. Numbering fewer than 400,000 out of a population of 23 million, they lack electoral weight; they are a minority in every city and county.

Most aborigines are Christians. Some indigenous groups were Christianized as long ago as the mid-seventeenth century, but many were not exposed to the Gospel until after World War II. The churches do not have the resources to alleviate the aborigines' economic woes, but their cultural activities play a vital role in preserving indigenous languages and traditions.

Many aborigines migrate to the lowland cities to work. A significant number end up doing menial jobs and living in illegal or marginal settlements. An aboriginal friend who has visited such places told me: "If the city government tears down the homes of these squatters, the people usually just return to the same spot a few days later. They don't have anywhere else to go. The apartments the government offers them are usually too expensive. So they just live in tents until they've rebuilt their shacks."

*   *   *

Chohlu in Hualien County lies close to the southeastern corner of Yushan National Park, and is inhabited by members of the Bunun tribe. The adolescents who horse around the village's basketball court are brown-skinned and round-eyed; many could pass for Indians or Nepalese. They enjoy an enviable environment – fresh air, a clean river, and verdant hills to the west. But they and their parents live in dreary gray blocks; traditional aboriginal architecture has disappeared from all but a handful of settlements.

Nanan, the final stop before the national park, is a tiny hamlet. The road is surfaced for a few more kilometers. It becomes a dirt track, then a narrow walking trail. The area is exceptionally rich in wildlife, especially monkeys, birds, butterflies, and insects.

Hikers often rest on a strategic ledge high above the Lakulaku River. A Japanese police station once stood there, part the colonial government's efforts to subdue the indigenous tribes. The Chinese imperial administration was content with a de facto partition of the island into two zones: the plains, inhabited by Han Chinese and pacified aboriginal communities, and what nineteenth-century map-makers labeled "savage territory" – a swath of mountains where armed head-hunters dwelt and which outsiders entered at great peril. Between 1739 and 1875, Han settlers were prohibited from entering aboriginal mountain districts; the ban was lifted to relieve population pressure on the lowlands. By contrast, the Japanese aggressively expanded the area under their control. Aborigines unwilling to submit to the new regime were pushed deeper and deeper into the mountains, and contained by a ring of electric fences and police outposts. Punitive expeditions were sent into areas of resistance, and schools set up to instill loyalty to the Japanese emperor.

Further along the same trail, a stone tablet erected by the Japanese commemorates the massacre of a police unit by aborigines in 1915. It is surprising that this monument has been allowed to stand: Many other vestiges of the Japanese colonial era – the *jinja* shrine atop Jade Mountain, and many graves – have been destroyed, desecrated or built over.

It took the Japanese most of their fifty years in Taiwan to grind the mountain people into submission. Several thousand policemen and soldiers were lost in the process, including 197 Japanese killed during the last major uprising, at Wushe (in what is now Nantou County) in 1930.

That rebellion ended with several hundred aboriginal warriors dead in their huts. According to the colonial government, the tribesmen hanged themselves when defeat became inevitable. Others say they were victims of poison-gas air raids. An English-language propaganda tome published in Tokyo a few years later (a copy of which I found in National Chengkung University's library) makes the bizarre claim that the Wushe revolt was "amicably suppressed."

*   *   *

We circumnavigated the police checkpoint and hitched a lift from a truck driver. Virtuous Moon and I were dropped off in Shenshan, a village in the northeastern corner of Pingtung County whose slate-roofed cottages are clustered tightly together as if in mutual defense. Our driver suggested we take a look at the Protestant church. It lacked a steeple, and resembled other single-story buildings in the village. But peering through the windows, we could see what made it noteworthy: The pews had been carved from immense blocks of wood to resemble rows of humans. The Rukai tribespeople who inhabit this valley are renowned for their carpentry and wood carving skills.

We hiked a few kilometers along the main road to the village of Wutai. It turned out to have a breathtaking setting on a steep hillside far above the valley floor. But for all the drama of its location, the village was somnolent. Barely a soul stirred. The police station seemed superfluous. The church was blandly utilitarian; behind it lay the village's one interesting landmark – a small, terraced graveyard. But Wutai lived up to its name: It means "fog plateau," and soon after midday a bank of thick mist rolled in.

There was an outbreak of activity as we sat resting on some concrete steps. The school day was over. Children played hopscotch and bought drinks from the village shop which, like

122

many others in the mountains, was run by Han Taiwanese. They waited with their teacher for the bus that would take them to their homes elsewhere in the valley. I was cross-examined as to my age, name, occupation and nationality. One little girl, obviously perplexed by my companion's darker than average complexion, round eyes and somewhat un-Chinese features, asked Virtuous Moon: "Are you from the lowlands?"

"Yes, I am. But lots of people on the plain think I am an aborigine."

Later, I asked Virtuous Moon if other people had mistaken her for an aborigine.

"When I was studying in Taipei, quite a few people asked me if I belonged to the Ami tribe or the Bunun tribe," she replied.

"What did you tell them?"

"Sometimes Ami, sometimes Bunun. Sometimes I told them the truth."

Beyond Ali, the final settlement, waterfalls spewed from the ridge above and crashed down onto the trail. The rivulets they created gurgled around our feet, then disappeared downwards into vegetation which had somehow taken root on the cliff. Squirrels bounded along the path; green lizards scampered in and out of the brambles. Had we kept walking eastward, the trail would have brought us to Little Ghost Lake, a small body of water 2,000 meters above sea level, and a destination whose name breaches the convention that every place in the Chinese world should have an optimistic label.

The following day we retraced our steps, then headed north along quiet mountain roads. At one spot we shared cold black tea with a group of workmen who were hammering slate into squares that could be sold. We came across tiny corn fields surrounded by crude palisades, and elsewhere glimpsed goats grazing by the roadside. Whenever a vehicle approached, the animals fled down perilous inclines.

By the middle of the afternoon we were close to what my

map called Swan Lake, but which a local referred to as Lovers' Lake. It turned out to be a circular pool about fifteen meters across, filled from one side by a waterfall, drained from the other by a rushing stream. There were no swans in sight, and previous visitors had left behind plenty of rubbish. But the water was a cooling blue, and the forest around it vigorously green. We pitched our tent, sweltered until the temperature dropped, and awoke the following morning to brilliant, dazzling sunshine.

A professional soldier driving a van down to the lowlands offered us a lift. I asked him if he was an aborigine: The vehemence of his denial was disturbing. Virtuous Moon had found being mistaken for a tribeswoman amusing; this man thought, perhaps, that any imputation of indigenous ancestry was an insult.

*   *   *

Head hunting continued until the 1920s. Bringing home a head was considered proof of one's maturity, and earned an aboriginal warrior respect in his tribe. The custom naturally intrigued nineteenth-century Western visitors, several of whom have written of encounters with bands of aborigines armed with spears, bows and matchlocks.

In *A Trip Into The Interior Of Formosa*, an account he wrote for the Royal Geographical Society, British consular official T.L. Bullock (later a professor of Chinese at Oxford University) reports: "The wild savages in Formosa seem to carry on the practice of man-hunting out of mere devilry and for the sake of obtaining skulls. They kill all alike, Chinese and aborigines... [hunting parties] lurk about the forest, sometimes cutting off a man working alone in his field, sometimes falling upon a band of travelers... When their provisions are exhausted, or they have obtained a head, they return home. In the latter case a feast is organized. The skull is roughly cleared out; wine is poured in, and it is handed round for the company to drink from."

During his 1873 expedition, Bullock came across a head-hunters' settlement high in the mountains. "Not long after we arrived, when strolling about the village and looking at what was to be seen, we discovered a row of skulls laid out on a raised board in front of one of the houses. There were no less than 25 of them, a few not yet bleached, others evidently many years old. We paid a good deal of attention to this display, and one of the party sat down and took a sketch of it. This, and our staring, put the savages into a bad and suspicious temper... to produce a better impression, we brought out some packets of needles and made presents from them to the women. Some men who had wounds or sores now applied to us for medical aid. Having a bottle of iodine, we painted the wounds with it, to the great satisfaction of our patients."

In an account dated 1877, George Taylor, a lighthouse keeper employed by the Imperial Chinese Maritime Customs Service, writes of finding a victim: "[As] we continued our journey, we found a little further on, on the banks of a small offshoot of the stream, the headless trunk of a Chinaman who could only have been killed two days previously. I insisted on the body being covered with sand, and, amid much grumbling at the fuss I made over what they considered a small matter, this was done."

Despite their passion for collecting heads, the aborigines seem not to have eaten their victims. Some Han settlers, however, showed no such qualms.

The Canadian Presbyterian missionary Mackay records coming across a crowd awaiting the execution of an aboriginal warrior, noting: "Scores were there on purpose to get parts of the body for food and medicine... the heart is eaten, flesh taken off in strips, and bones boiled to a jelly and preserved as a specific for malarial fever."

In *The Island Of Formosa; Past and Present; History,*

People, Resources and Commercial Prospects, James W. Davidson, the first US consul stationed in Taiwan, writes: "One horrible feature of the campaign against the savages was the sale by the Chinese in open market of savage flesh. Impossible as it may seem that a race with such high pretensions to civilization and religion should be guilty of such barbarity, yet such is the truth. After killing a savage, the head was commonly severed from the body and exhibited to those who were not on hand to witness the prior display of slaughter and mutilation. The body was then either divided among its captors and eaten, or sold... The kidney, liver, heart, and soles of the feet were considered the most desirable portions, and were ordinarily cut up into very small pieces, boiled and eaten somewhat in the form of soup... The Chinese profess to believe, in accordance with an old superstition, that the eating of savage flesh will give them strength and courage... During the outbreak of 1891, savage flesh was brought in – in baskets – the same as pork, and sold like pork in the markets of Tokoham before the eyes of all, foreigners included..."

THE EAST

The first time I took a train from Taipei to Ilan, the lush greenness of much of the northeast pleased me, but I was shocked by the despoiled, brutalized appearance of industrial Hsichih.

The island's north and northeast coasts are soaked with rain for the greater part of each year. The region is even more luxuriant than south and central Taiwan. But there is little in the way of flat land, so rice fields are few and far between, and orchards less common than betel nut stands. Every crag is wrapped in thick foliage; the landscape is riven by streams and gorges. The scenery is dramatic, but hardly inviting. Were it not for the copper, coal and gold hereabouts, few Han settlers would have made their homes north of Taipei.

In Juifang, a town that once served as a center of the mining industry, many older buildings have tarpaper roofs to keep out the rain. Instead of the gray cement horseshoe-shaped graves so common in the south, here the dead are entombed beneath garish structures which resemble tiny temples. Compared with the lavish cemeteries, the town itself lacks color, and has an impoverished air about it.

South of Juifang, the former coal-mining villages served by the Pinghsi Branch Railroad have been severely depressed for years. Many of their inhabitants – like those of rust-belt towns in Western countries – have moved to places where jobs are easier to find. The rail line was built more than a century ago by a company which extracted coal from the hills east of Taipei. The mines were abandoned after World War II, though decrepit coal sheds and sealed-off workings can be seen from the train. Remarkably enough, the upper stretch of the Keelung River – which broadens and blackens as its approaches the capital – looks fairly clean as it passes Shihfen. This area, known for its waterfalls, attracts anglers and hikers.

The train to Ilan passes through a two-kilometer-long tunnel before emerging a stone's throw from the Pacific Ocean. This side of the island always seems sunnier and healthier. With fewer people and less industry, the air quality is better. There is much less congestion; the pace of life is altogether slower.

Unless it is raining, 2,000-meter-high mountains are visible to the southwest of Ilan. One time, before heading into the highlands, I wandered around this small city, and into a traditional morning market. Tarpaulins stretched out to block the sunshine gave the place a souk-like atmosphere. But rather than mounds of exotic spices, more prosaic items provided color: cheap plastic goods, tinned products, and children's clothes. Housewives on 50-cc scooters weaved between shoppers; one section seemed to be a drive-through wet market. But I saw nothing I wished to buy, so I went into a small supermarket to get provisions for my trip.

There it struck me that foreigners visiting Taiwan – especially those traveling through areas such as Ilan, where very little English is spoken – should be thankful for one small mercy if nothing else: Most merchandise is labeled in English as well as Chinese characters.

This is true even for goods clearly not destined for the international marketplace: cans of asparagus juice; packets of tiny dried fish mixed with almonds; obscure brands of instant noodles. Few local companies bother to have the English on their products proofread (this is obvious from the misspellings), because the labeling is not added for the convenience of foreign shoppers. Many businesses, I suspect, add English words to their products not so much in the hope of winning export orders, but to impress local customers. In Japan, which receives far more foreign visitors than Taiwan, this ploy is not much used: Japanese consumers perhaps have greater faith in their nation's manufactures. (A friend working for an advertising company told me that some Taiwan firms go so far as to give themselves names crafted to look like they were translated from a foreign language.)

Having stocked up I decided to call a friend. To reach the nearest payphone I had to clamber through a tangle of folding tables and plastic stools. The device wore a crust of grime – residues from a nearby fried-food stall. I decided not to bother with my call. Ilan is one of my favorite places, and one of the cleanest and most livable cities on the island, but my tolerance for urban Taiwan was under strain. I was glad to be leaving the lowlands.

*   *   *

Lishan, near the midpoint of the Central Cross-Island Highway, is surrounded by impressive mountain scenery, but parts of this high-altitude district are shanty-town ugly. Farmers' shacks made of plastic sheeting and corrugated iron dot the hills above Techi Reservoir, while the village itself consists of unsightly cement buildings.

Farming has had a demoralizing effect on the landscape. The lower flanks of Taiwan's mountains are typically covered with dense forest. (The summits are grassy or rocky, depending how steep they are.) But the hillsides around Lishan have been denuded, planted with fruit trees, and cobwebbed with nets to keep off birds. Plastic water pipes crisscross the valley, and the smell of smoke – whatever is pruned is burned – is everywhere.

*   *   *

In Hualien I alarmed two Mormon missionaries – white Americans in their early twenties – by badgering them with questions.

I wanted to know if their church's free English classes attracted many people. ("Lots of people come once or twice, but very few turn up regularly.") I inquired if the Mormon custom of baptizing converts' ancestors was an impediment to their proselytizing efforts, and if there had been any cases where clan elders had taken action to stop lineage records falling into the hands of converts. (Both men hedged, saying they had nothing to do with posthumous baptisms.) And I asked if the injunction against tea was an obstacle, given the drink's popularity in Chinese societies. (Not for those sincere in their search for truth, they told me.)

Whatever their religion's rules on tea or ancestors, the physical appearance of most Mormon missionaries surely helps attract converts. All of them dress neatly. Most, including these two men, are effusively healthy – living, breathing advertisements for the non-smoking, non-drinking, no-caffeine lifestyle endorsed by Mormonism. I was reminded of the young Tainan woman who, years earlier, had asked me why the Mormons she had met were so much more handsome and wholesome than the dissolute young Westerners who taught English in the language school she attended.

Later I stepped into a ferociously air-conditioned fast-food eatery. It felt like changing continents. The place's youthful clientele were busy stuffing burgers and French fries into their mouths, poring over textbooks, or napping. There was not a grain of rice nor a chopstick to be seen.

Just as I was finishing my meal, a girl asked me in English if I could spare her a few minutes. I said I could. She then beckoned four friends over. These girls – all of them were about eighteen, fashionably attired and immaculately groomed – had been ordered by their high school English teacher to interview as many foreigners as they could find. The questions were ones I had answered hundreds of times before, yet the girls were so faultlessly charming that I was happy to help. At the end of the interview all five stood up and thanked me: Their leader proffered her hand. When I stood up I towered over her, and my fist enveloped her slim hand. She teetered backwards. I must have struck her as a gangling, acromegalic giant.

*   *   *

When I awoke, breakfast vendors were taking up positions along the narrow street beneath my window. On each of the stainless steel trolleys a tub of hot soybean milk breathed steam. Eggs were cracked open, fried and formed into pancakes. Savory doughnut sticks were batched upright like the wooden prognostication lots I had seen the day before in one of Hualien's temples. Somewhere in the neighborhood a revving scooter heralded the morning rush hour.

I decided to head further south, to where the east coast seethes with geothermal energy. Local and Japanese tourists are drawn to these hot emissions of sulfurous water. Foremost among the resort spas is Chihpen, just south of Taitung. The three public pools – one cool, one warm, the third scalding – are shaded by trees. Cold water shoots from a pipe suspended above the largest of these pools, massaging the shoulders of those who stand beneath.

Chihpen's clientele are a motley lot: boisterous aboriginal kids, local Han Taiwanese families, and Taipei residents conspicuous by their pallor and tidy dress. On one visit I was buttonholed by a man whose close-cropped hair and swirling tattoos suggested a criminal background. He offered me a can of beer, and brooked no refusal. Another time I watched as a doddering old man, most probably in his eighties, was tenderly assisted into the water by a couple I took to be his son and daughter-in-law.

A short distance south of Chihpen there is another spa, known by its aboriginal name of Bilu. The springs here were once earmarked for development, but those plans seem to have been abandoned. The road leading to it crosses a small bridge, then ends. Only hikers and four-wheel-drive vehicles can reach the springs. The natural state of Bilu counterpoints the feverish development prevailing elsewhere in Taiwan. For this reason I hope it can be preserved as it is.

*   *   *

It is possible to traverse the entire length of the Southern Cross-Island Highway by bus, but on one occasion I decided to hitch hike.

After detraining at Chihshang – the paddies that encircle this tiny town are reputed to produce some of the best rice in Taiwan – I walked until I found a straight stretch of road where soliciting a ride was less likely to cause an accident. There I set my pack down, and contemplated the scenery until onward transportation presented itself. Westerners hitching in Taiwan need never wait very long.

I had a whole day to get to Tainan and wanted to maximize my time in the highlands. So I told the first man to offer me a ride that I was heading no further than the aboriginal village of Litao.

The eastern half of the Southern Cross-Island Highway is slowly becoming less spectacular. Hair-raising curves are being replaced with straight tunnels; concrete shelters cover the stretches most vulnerable to landslides. But it remains one of the most beautiful mountain roads in Taiwan – which has many beautiful mountain roads – and should be on every visitor's itinerary. For long stretches it winds high above the Hsinwu River, a crooked blue channel full of huge white boulders, and in places narrows almost to the width of a single vehicle.

Like many of the villages which abut Taiwan's national parks, Litao – despite the clean air and excellent views – is not an especially attractive place to live. The housing is of poor quality, and there are few facilities. Several mountain settlements have elementary schools, but no resident doctor, and rely on medical teams who visit once a week.

Returning to the main road from Litao, I made my excuses when a betel-nut-addled truck driver stopped and offered me transport all the way to Tainan; he looked like he would be a terror awheel. Not so the next man, a young school teacher who had been visiting friends in Taitung.

We stopped to enjoy the air at Yakou, at 2,500 meters above sea level the highest point on the highway. We gazed southward over beautiful tracts of forest, so inaccessible that loggers have yet exploit them. To the northeast stood the bleak, crumbling flanks of Hsiangyangshan, while a dab of cloud sat atop Kuanshan, a mountain which forms part of the watershed boundary between east and west Taiwan. I have hiked to its bald, flat summit three or four times, and when looking back down at the highway – from that perspective it is no more than a tiny notch cut into the hillside – have enjoyed the insignificance of humanity in this part of Taiwan.

The Southern Cross-Island Highway, and Yakou in particular, is as good a place as any to see a peculiarly Taiwanese phenomena: Tour buses whose passengers draw the curtains and ignore much of the scenery they are passing – but sit up and stare as soon as a Westerner is spotted. During vacations this route becomes hopelessly clogged with sightseers. But more dispiriting than the traffic jams are the piles of trash that cover the roadsides: wrappers, cans, packets and cigarette butts – items people could easily carry away and dispose of properly. It astonishes me more than it angers me to think that people drive so far to enjoy nature's splendor, then thoughtlessly despoil it. (Many of those who live in the mountains behave no better. In several villages there is a despicable tendency to dispose of garbage by hurling it over the nearest cliff. Sometimes, when pausing on a bridge to take in the view, I would see in the gully below old furniture, or even the remains of a stove or refrigerator.)

Between Litao and Tienchih, the damage wrought by landslides was evident in many places. The white safety wall was chipped like a set of bad teeth. At one spot a small part of the road had disappeared, like the broken lip of a plate. My driver looked tense as he eased past, but he agreed when I said the scenery made such difficulties worth enduring.

At Tienchih (which means "Heaven's Pond") there is a pretty pool, and a wooden police station. The latter watches over the former, which sometimes attracts religious eccentrics whose spirit-money burning activities endanger the surrounding forest. West of the police station the road drops sharply. The weather began to deteriorate. For a few minutes clouds melted beautifully down the mountainside. I glimpsed wizened alpine trees, sodden in the mist, and a motorcyclist scrambling to put on a plastic poncho; then all was lost to rain.

*　　　　*　　　　*

Back in Ilan, I wandered through a night market. At dusk scores of vendors appropriated a street near the city's only department store, and within an hour the thoroughfare was filled with parents and their children, young couples, and clusters of innocent-looking teenagers. Most of the under-50s – men and women alike – wore T-shirts, short pants and plastic sandals. I could easily believe what I had read: That in the days before air-conditioning and cable TV, night markets were especially popular with working-class families eager to escape their cramped dwellings and enjoy some cheap snacks.

Every few meters people were selling something. With few

exceptions, the goods were cheap, dubious, shoddy, or tacky. The selection ranged from Buddha statuettes to soft-porn VCDs. One man tried to sell me a crystal bracelet the color of a chain-smoker's teeth; another interrupted his Taiwanese sales spiel to greet me in English, while a third vendor was alerted to my presence by his dumbfounded infant daughter. I made way for an elderly man maneuvering a freight-carrying tricycle through the crowd. He inched forward patiently, greeted an acquaintance, then disappeared down a side alley.

I sought out the food area. Industriousness was evident all around me. Cooks stirred with fearless determination as flames shot up from beneath their clattering woks, or puffed on cigarettes while nudging shellfish omelets across grease-encrusted hot plates. Kitchen hands dripped sweat while slicing vegetables or ladling soup. Serving was done with speed rather than panache; spills were wiped up matter-of-factly.

As at every night market I've been to, disposable bowls, plates and chopsticks were the norm. Those who wanted to sit had to make do with plastic stools and folding tables. Most customers stood up the moment they swallowed the last mouthful, their places immediately taken by those who'd been waiting. This no-frills, fast food approach to business is one reason why outdoor eating in Taiwan is so cheap. But many Western visitors are too squeamish to enjoy night-market food.

I saw barbecued cobs of corn daubed with spicy sauce; sausages enlivened with a squirt of wasabe; and spicy tofu served with glistening cubes of congealed ducks' blood. One place served pork ribs – bowlfuls of crudely chopped gray bones eaten with rice. And from a vendor who sold nothing else, I ordered a bowl of the local specialty: Yuanshan Fish Ball Noodle Soup.

I elected to eat sitting down: This meant enduring blasts of heat from the stove in front of me, and shoves from behind as passers-by requested takeouts. Coins and plastic bags full of hot soup were exchanged over my head; cooking vapors and the smell of fresh sweat assailed my nose; a legless unfortunate, begrimed from head to stump, dragged himself along the ground and tugged at my arm in the hope I would buy a handtowel from him out of pity.

I watched the young, long-haired beauty across from me. After lapping up a serving of stinky tofu, she chewed on some deep-fried chicken, then spat bones onto the table. Even after years in Taiwan, scenes like this – or super-fashionable Taipei office ladies buying chickens' feet, ducks' heads or other repulsive comestibles – still beguile me. The *nouveau riche* businessman who double-parks his BMW, plunks himself down on a wooden bench before a roadside stall, and devours a bowl of noodles elbow-to-elbow with factory hands and construction workers, represents a refreshing classlessness. The sight of a dead pig being transported on the back of a motorcycle, its trotters dragging on the blacktop, is compelling rather than disgusting. The blind old man in a night market who plucks at his lute, then gropes for coins in a tin pot, should arouse more pity than curiosity. But before I consider how he came to be there, and what his life might be like, my attention always shifts to some other spectacle. And there is always some other spectacle.

Wherever I travel in Taiwan, some people react to my presence with stares, pointed fingers, or exclamations. But I can hardly complain: Just as many Taiwanese see me as an amusing or frightful distraction, I have always regarded the extremes of beauty and ugliness on this island as an entertainment – a freak show, almost – guaranteeing that I should never feel bored. Rather than be put off by the everchanging grotesquerie, as many foreign visitors are, I chose to be enthralled by the human and natural wonders, the color, vigor, and excitement.